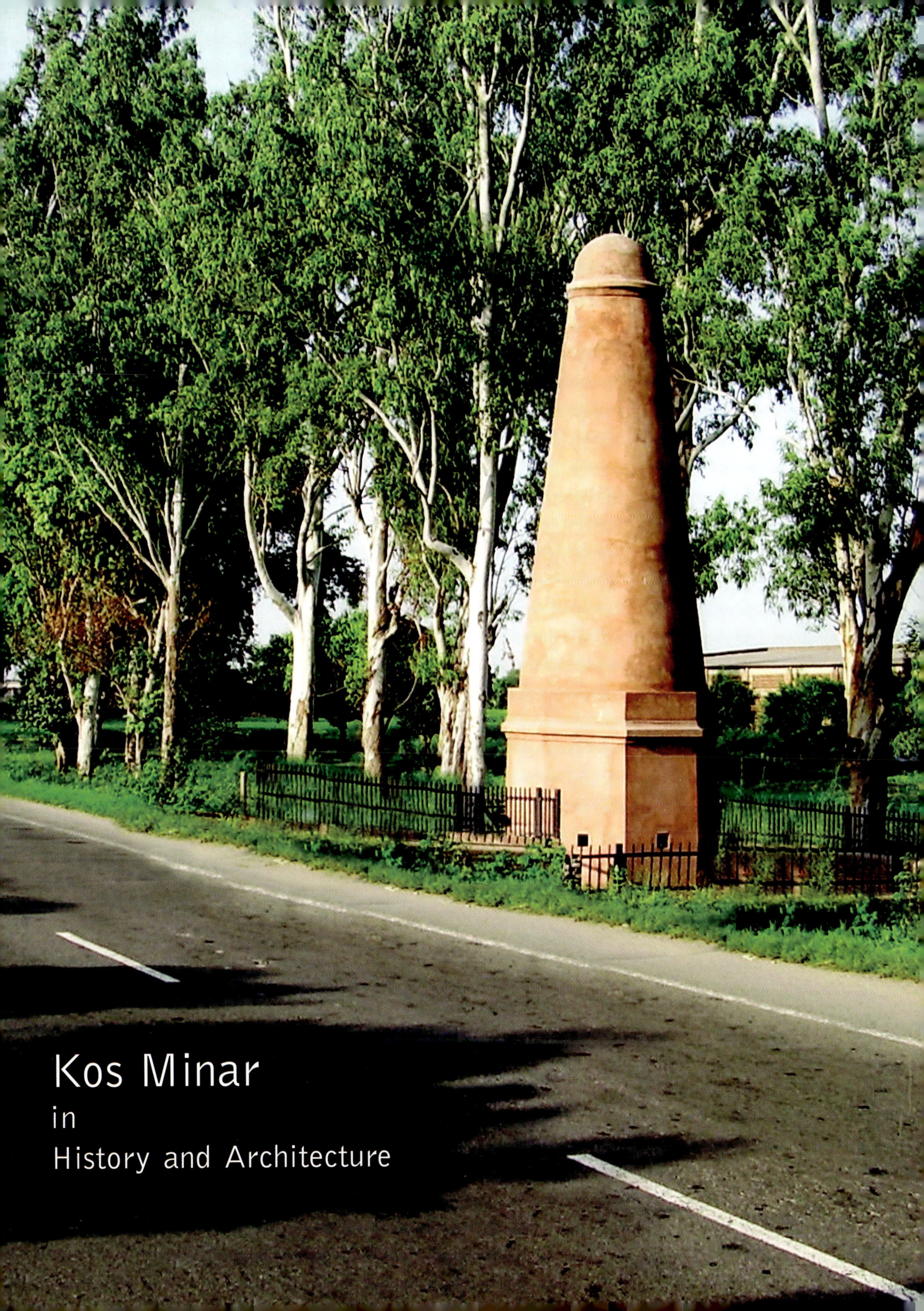

Kos Minar in History and Architecture

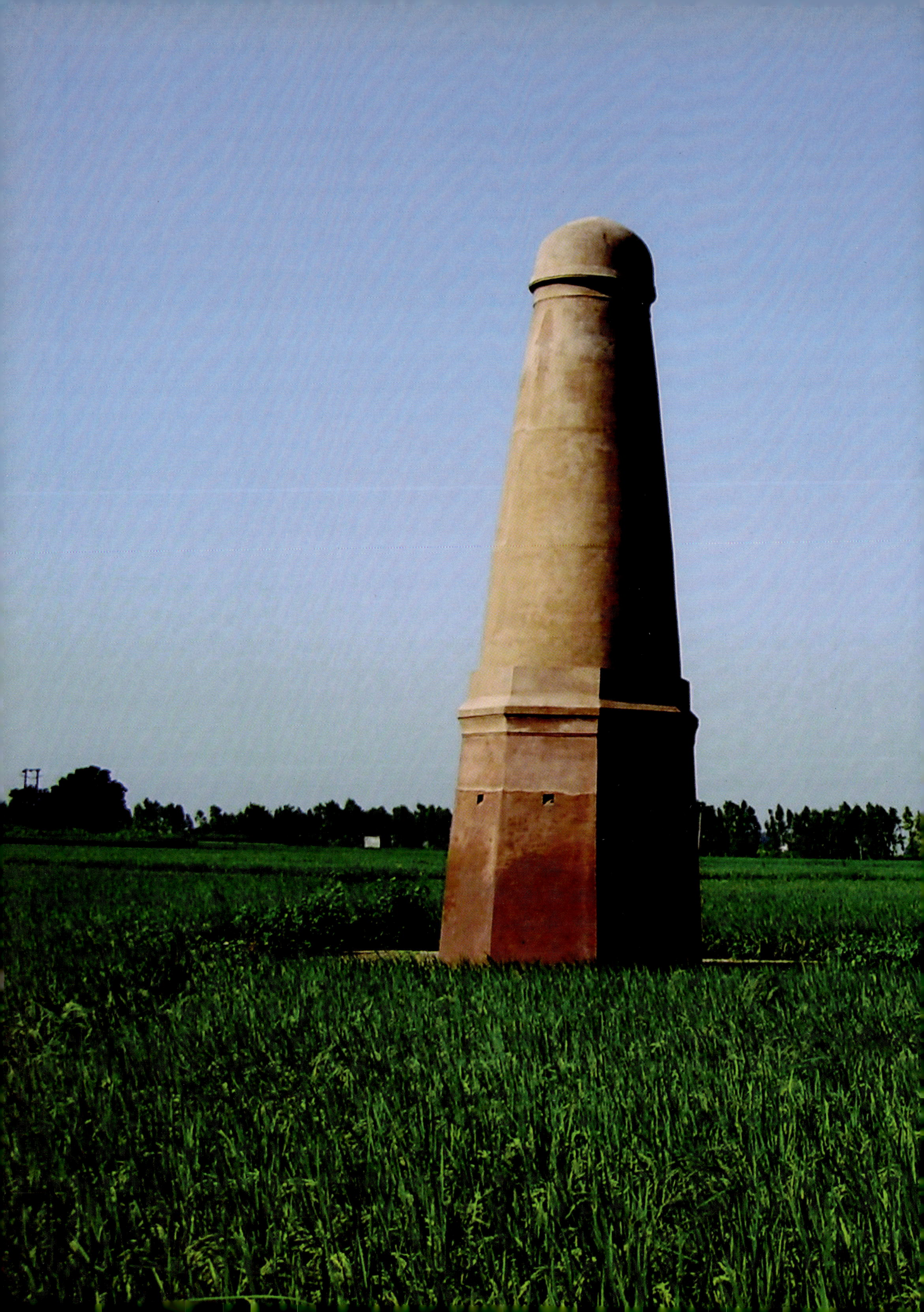

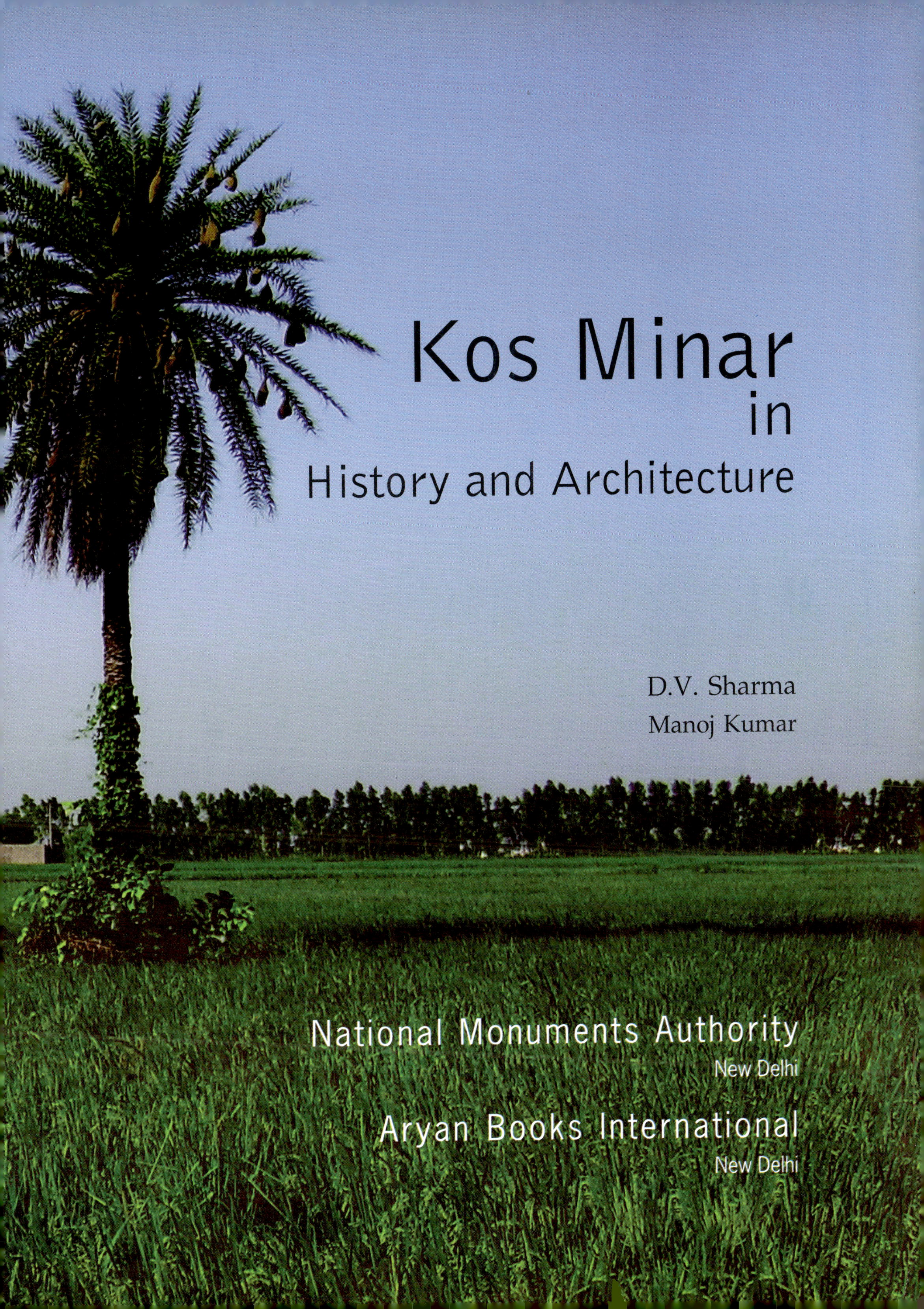

Kos Minar in History and Architecture

D.V. Sharma
Manoj Kumar

National Monuments Authority
New Delhi

Aryan Books International
New Delhi

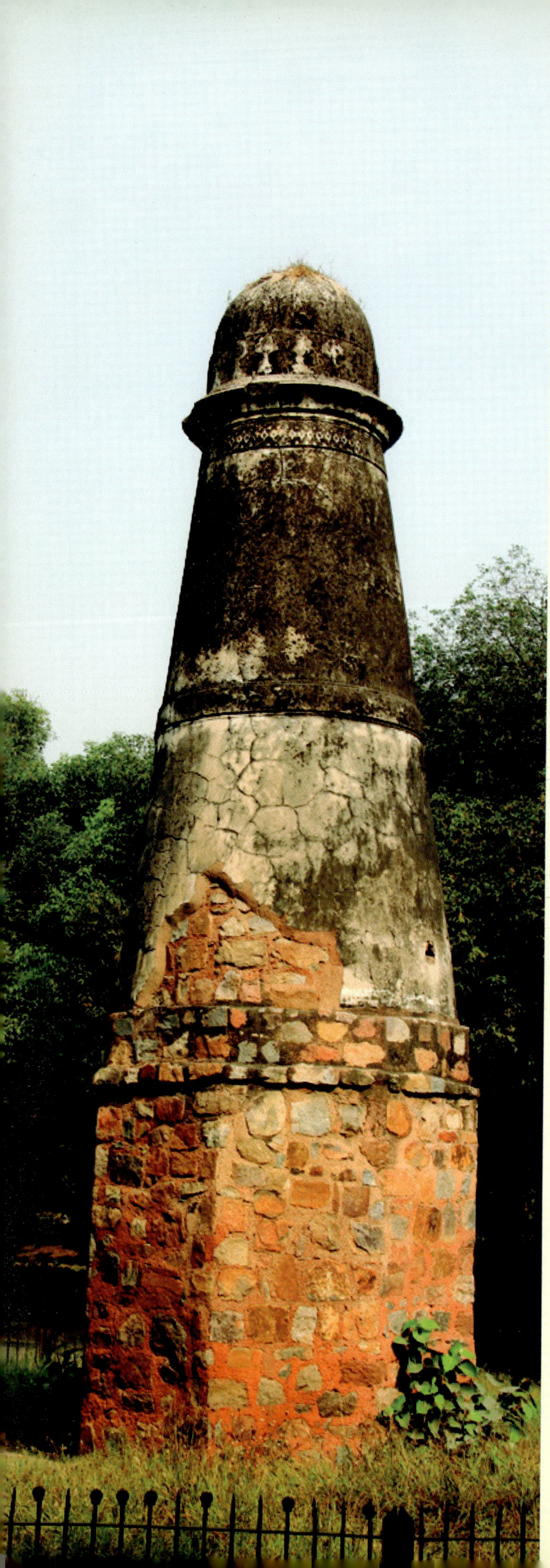

Kos Minar in History and Architecture

ISBN: 978-81-7305-445-7 (HB)
978-81-7305-446-4 (PB)

First Published in **2013** by

National Monuments Authority
24, Tilak Marg, New Delhi - 110 001
www.nma.gov.in

in association with

Aryan Books International
Pooja Apartments, 4B, Ansari Road, New Delhi-110 002
Tel.: 23287589, 23255799; Fax: 91-11-23270385
E-mail: aryanbooks@gmail.com
www.aryanbooks.co.in

Computer Typeset and Printed in India at
ABI Prints & Publishing Co., New Delhi.

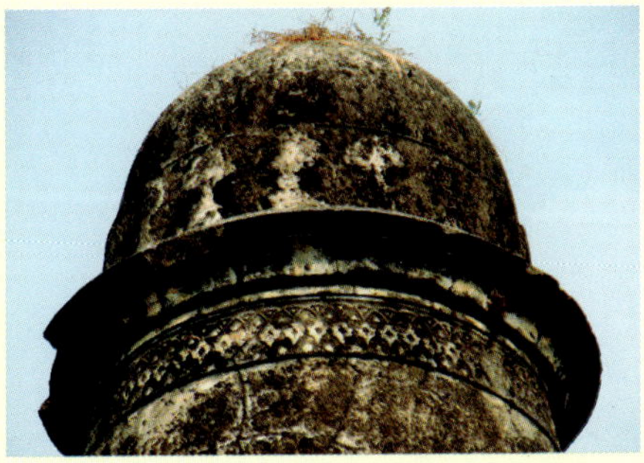

Dedicated to

Unheard Unsung Populace of Hindustan
Who Contributed in Countless Ways
for
Maintenance and Upkeep
of
National Communication Systems for Centuries

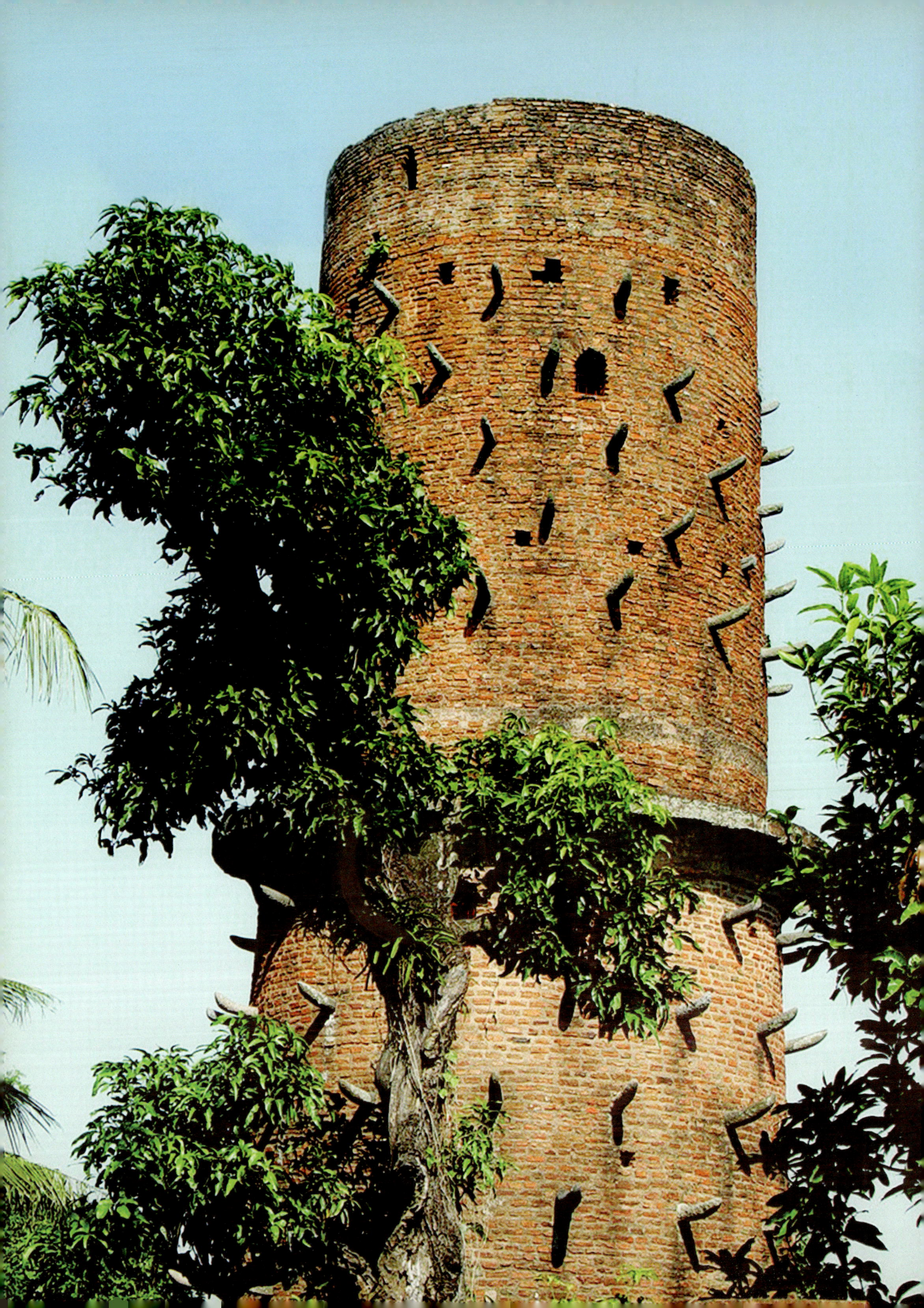

Foreword

Historically renowned seven cities of Delhi has been conglomeration of three hundred and sixty five rural villages. The archaeological remains are found scattered in these villages, but unfortunately in the process of rapid urbanisation, several monuments of immense historical importance have been lost forever. The rural villages that constitute Delhi have lost their original character and are almost transformed beyond recognition. The property speculation and real estate development causing such urbanisation leads to high density of permanent structures which are adversely affecting future potential of archaeological significance of the city.

The Ancient Monuments Archaeological Sites and Remains (AMASR) Act 1958 (Amendment and Validation 2010) has strengthened the legal framework for protection of monuments and sites of national importance. The National Monuments Authority (NMA) has been constituted to regulate development and construction activity in the vicinity of monuments that fall under the statutory provisions of the above Act.

NMA, in addition to its regulatory powers, is involved in the process of carrying out research and documentation to prepare a comprehensive and updated database for implementation of regulatory measures on the ground, as per provisions of the AMASR Act. This research monograph is part of an ongoing process in the operation of NMA, and is intended to serve as a future guide to govern the course of planning and heritage bye-laws that respect ancient and historic character of urban villages and areas around protected monuments.

The Kos Minars in India comprise a lesser known but highly significant component of our heritage stock, as a standing representation of sophisticated communication networks of our glorious past. However, there is a dearth of meaningful understanding on the significance of such type of monument. In re-interpreting Chor Minar in Delhi, NMA technical team throws new light on this important but less-understood relic of medieval India.

(Pravin Srivastava)
National Monuments Authority

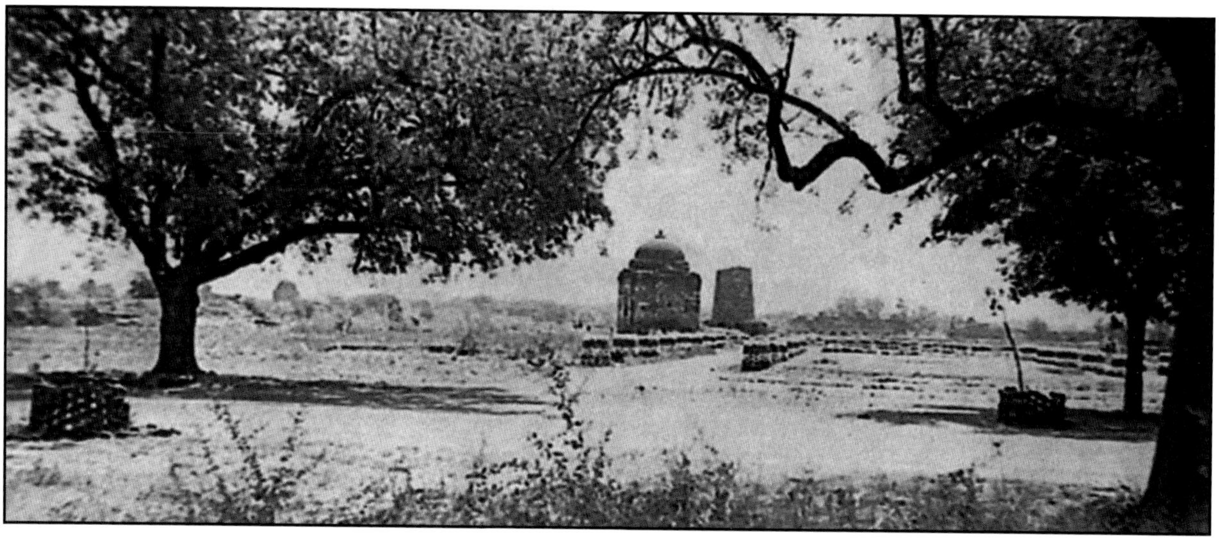

An archival photograph (c. 1950) of Chor Minar with adjoining tomb demolished due to urbanisation of Kharera village, presently known as Hauz Khas Enclave.

Acknowledgements

We are grateful to Maulvi Zafar Hasan, Prof. Moti Chandra, Prof. B.B. Lal, Prof. R. Nath, Dr. Y.D. Sharma and Dr. Subhash Parihar, whose scholarly works have been utilised in present research monograph elaborately. Some drawings, field data and photographs from Archaeological Survey of India (ASI) and Deptt. of Archaeology, Govt. of Delhi were of immense help in this context. We are also thankful to Prof. Himanshu Prabha Ray, Chairperson, National Monuments Authority (NMA) for valuable suggestions and guidance. The officers and staff of the NMA have encouraged us during research work and we are specially grateful to Mr. Saptarshi Sanyal and Ms. Shampa Chakraborty for their help and support. Above all, we are indebted to Archaeological Survey of India, a premier Government organization involved in multi-disciplinary research activities on heritage of mankind since 1861. In fact, we have learnt several ways of unveiling our glorious past from this organization, and would continue to do so in future.

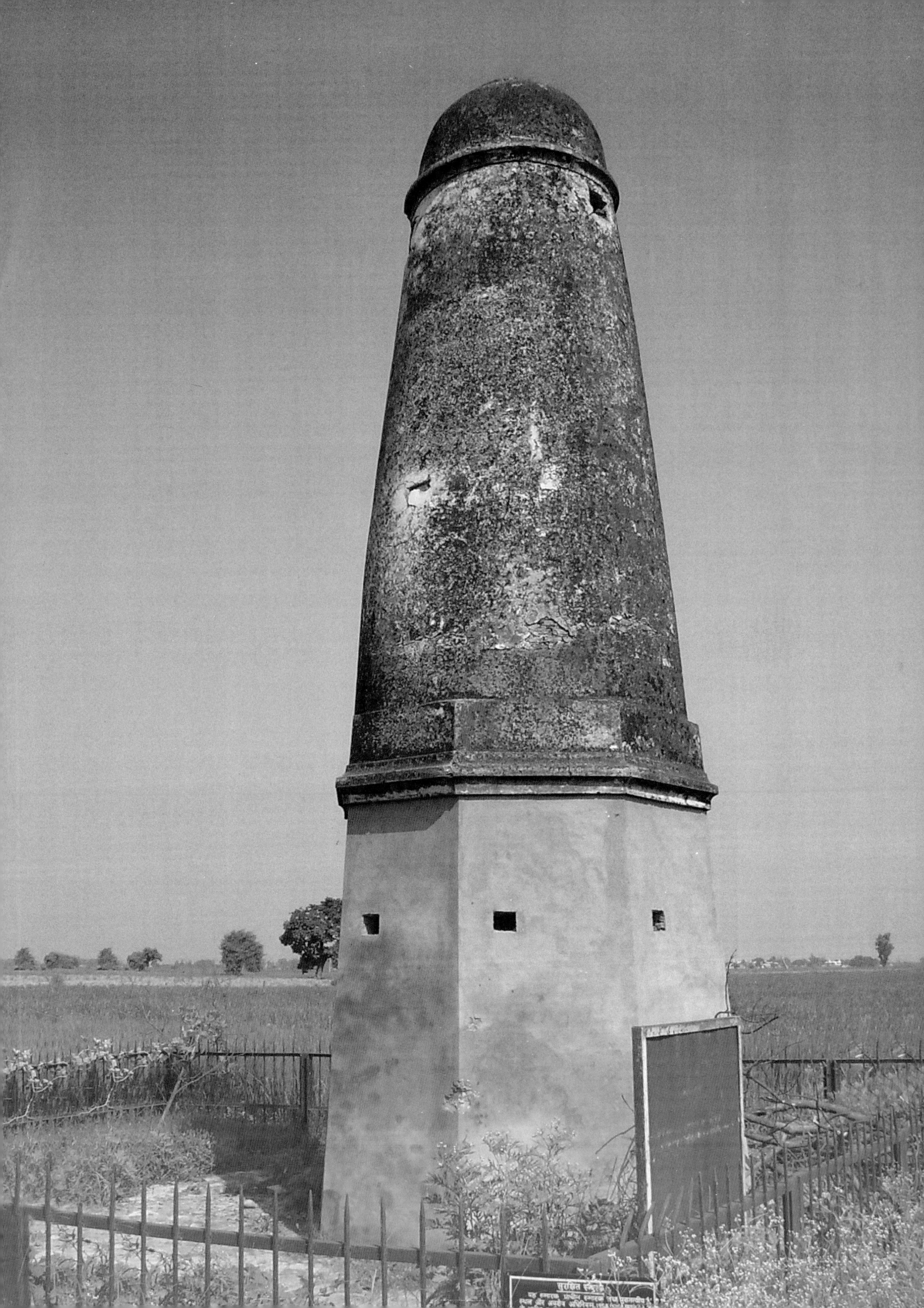

Contents

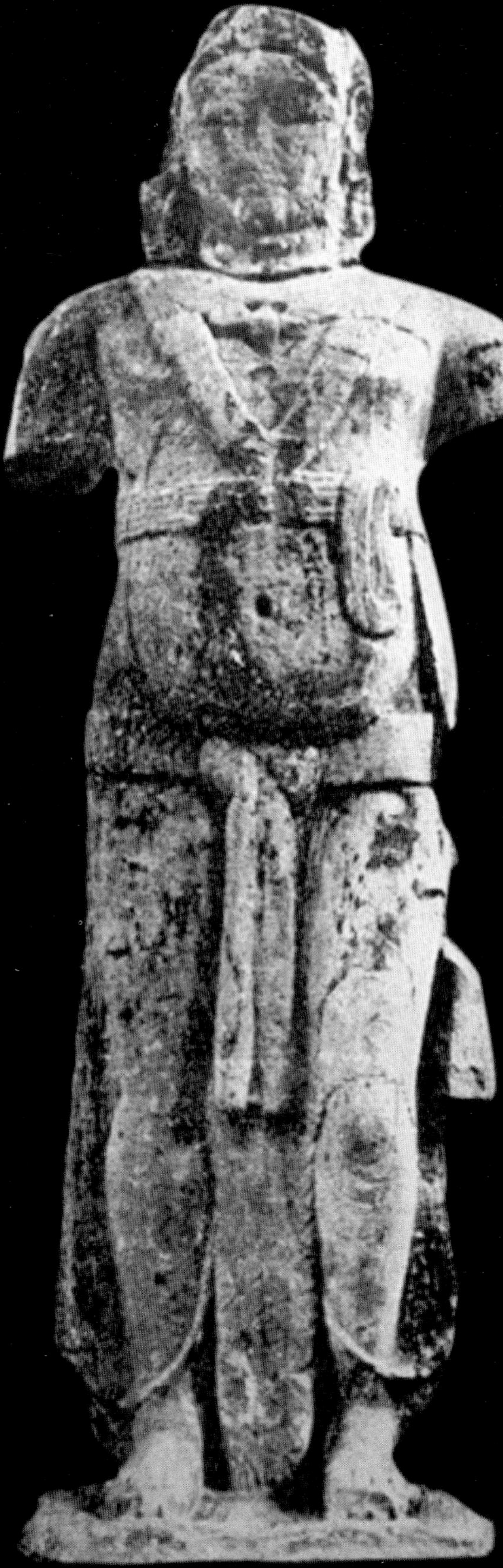

Manibhadra Yaksha, Parkham, 2nd century BC, presiding deity of land-route traders (after Moti Chandra 1977).

List of Illustrations

Page No.

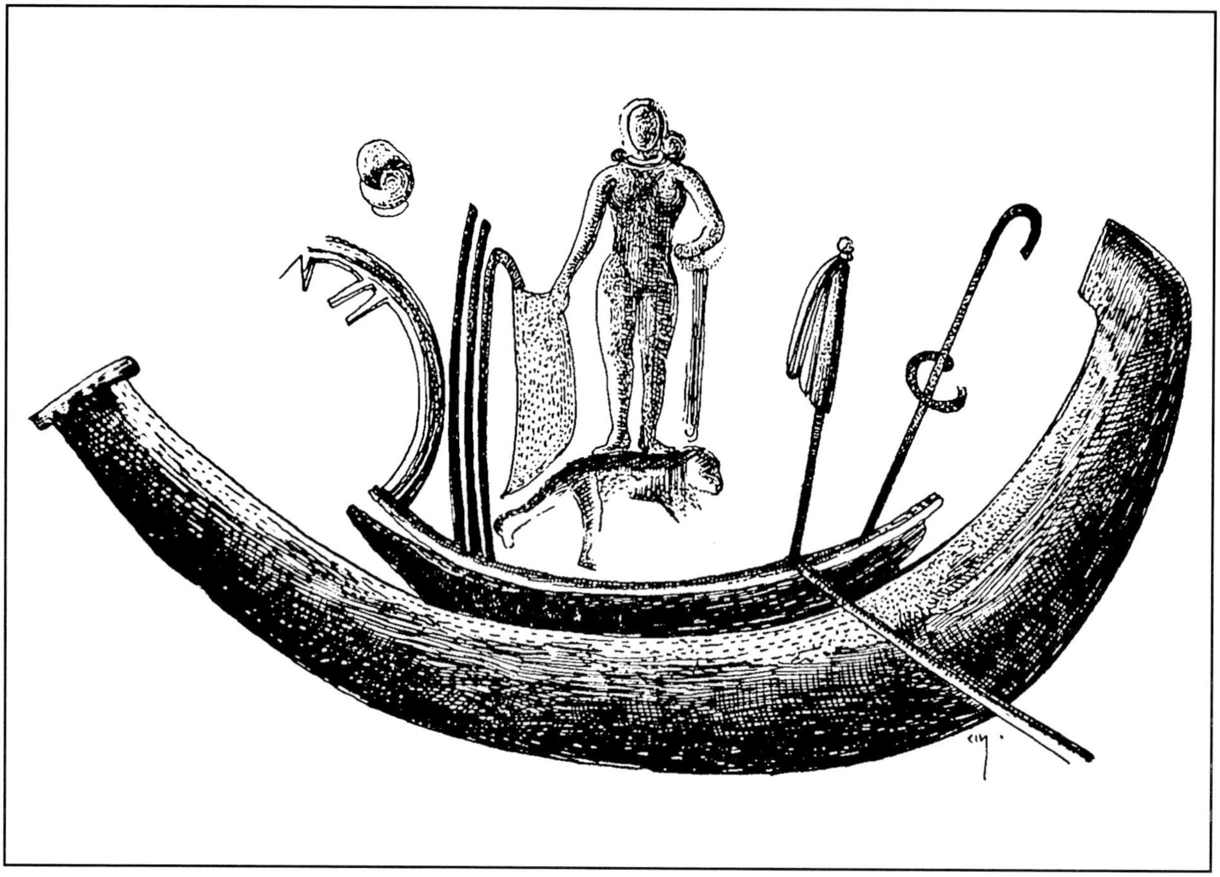

Manimekhala, Basard (Vaishali), 5th century AD, terracotta seal, presiding deity of seafaring traders (after Moti Chandra 1977).

1 Introduction

The ancient routes *Uttarapath*, *Dakshinapath*, Silk Route and few passes (Khyber, Bolan and Gomal) to India contributed significant historical achievements not only for trade purpose and pilgrimage alone, but also for the ruler's and army's travels for campaign and hunting expeditions.[1] Since time immemorial, the traders, striders and invaders undertook journeys and kept above routes operational even beyond the boundaries of Indian empire. The *Uttarapath*, *Dakshinapath* and Silk Route, no doubt, remained prime means of all communications. Besides religious propagation and trade, merchants or caravans used above routes with carts, asses, horses, mules, camels, palanquins or even as pedestrians, in favourable or odd situations (Fig. 1).

In this context, ancient religious text of Parsis is thought provoking and offers better proposition. The first *Frakart* (Chapter) of *Avesta* (Persian Religious Text) is an enumeration of the 16 countries of the earth created by *Ahura Mazda*. It explains the sequence from the first to the sixteen best countries and concludes that "these are more lovely, marvelous and praise-worthy towns and countries." It is a "moral introduction to geography" and begins with Airyana Vaejah (Eranvez). It is the first best country, elysium to which all mankind wants to emigrate. 2. Soghd (Greek Sogdiana), 3. Marv, 4. Balkh (Greek Bactria), 5. Nisya (Nisa, lay between Balkh and Marv), 6. Harirud,

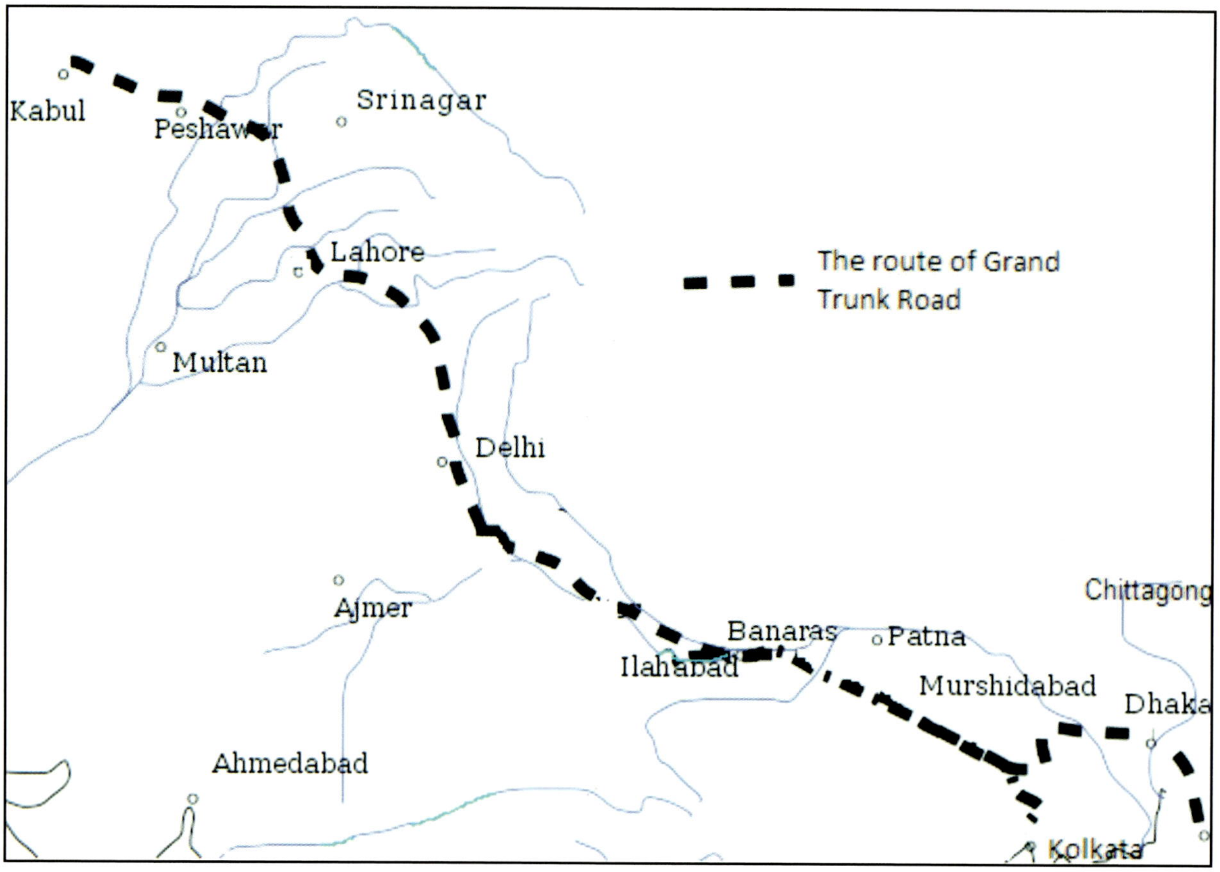

Fig. 1. Physical map of ancient trade route from Sonargaon to Iran.

7. Kabul or Gandhar (Persian name Kapul), 8. Mesene, 9. Gurgan, 10. Kandahar or Quandahar, 11. Hilmand, 12. Rai, 13. Khurasan , 14. Kirman, 15. Hapta Hendu (Vedic Sapta Sindhava, Sindh, a name of the Indus country or India), 16. Land adjoining the source of the Ranha, the name of the country which was Republic.[2]

Another relevant reference in this context is in the *Baudhayana Srautasutra* (18.44:397.9 sqq), a vedic text. The English translation is as follows "Ayu migrated eastwards. His (people) are the *Kuru-Panchalas* and *Kasi-Videhas*. This is the Ayava (migration). Amavasu migrated westwards. His (people) are the *Gandhari*, *Parasu* and *Aratta*. This is the Amavasava (migration)."[3] (Aila Pururavas and Urvasi had two sons and the passage contains dialogue between them which refers to the horse, chariot parts, hundred houses and hundred jars of ghee). The above textual reference throws ample light on ancient routes, geography and movement of the people in 6th century BC (Fig. 4).

The Mauryan Emperor Ashok (3rd century BC) consolidated and initiated ancient routes originating from his capital city Pataliputra and subsequentlyfor

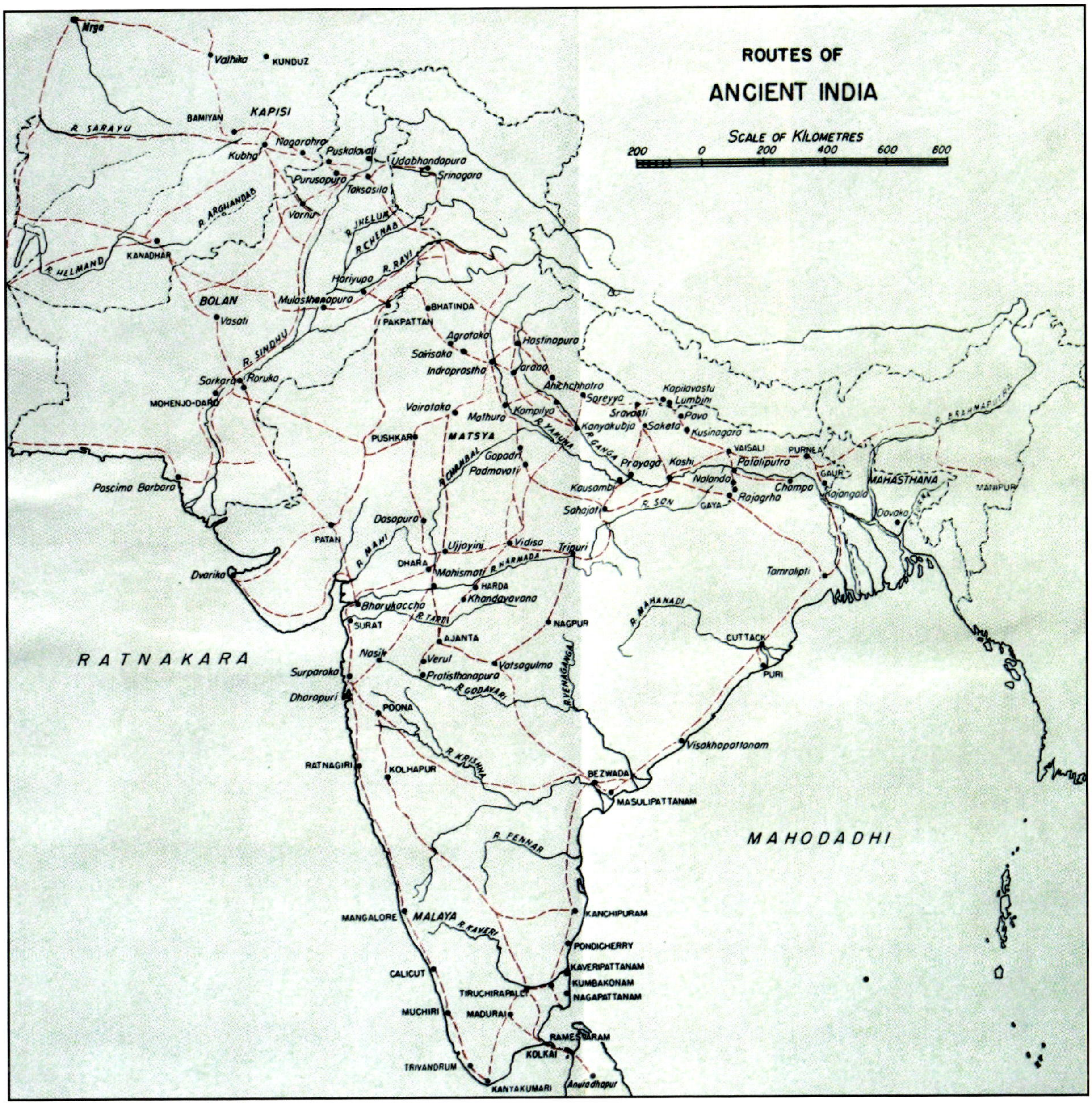

Fig. 2. Routes of Ancient India.

several centuries, it has linked the eastern and western regions of the Indian subcontinent, running from Howrah, West Bengal in India, across north India, in Peshawar (now in Pakistan) up to Kabul, Afghanistan and further to Balkh (Bactria, in Central Asia) respectively (Fig. 5). He ordered to plant trees on either side of the roads for convenience of the travellers, and provided facilities of wells, stepwells, tanks, bridges, inns, hospitals (for animals and human) along the road to ensure safety and comfortable journey. It was in accordance with *Purusharth Chatusya* (*Dharma*, *Artha*, *Kama*, *Moksha*) as state

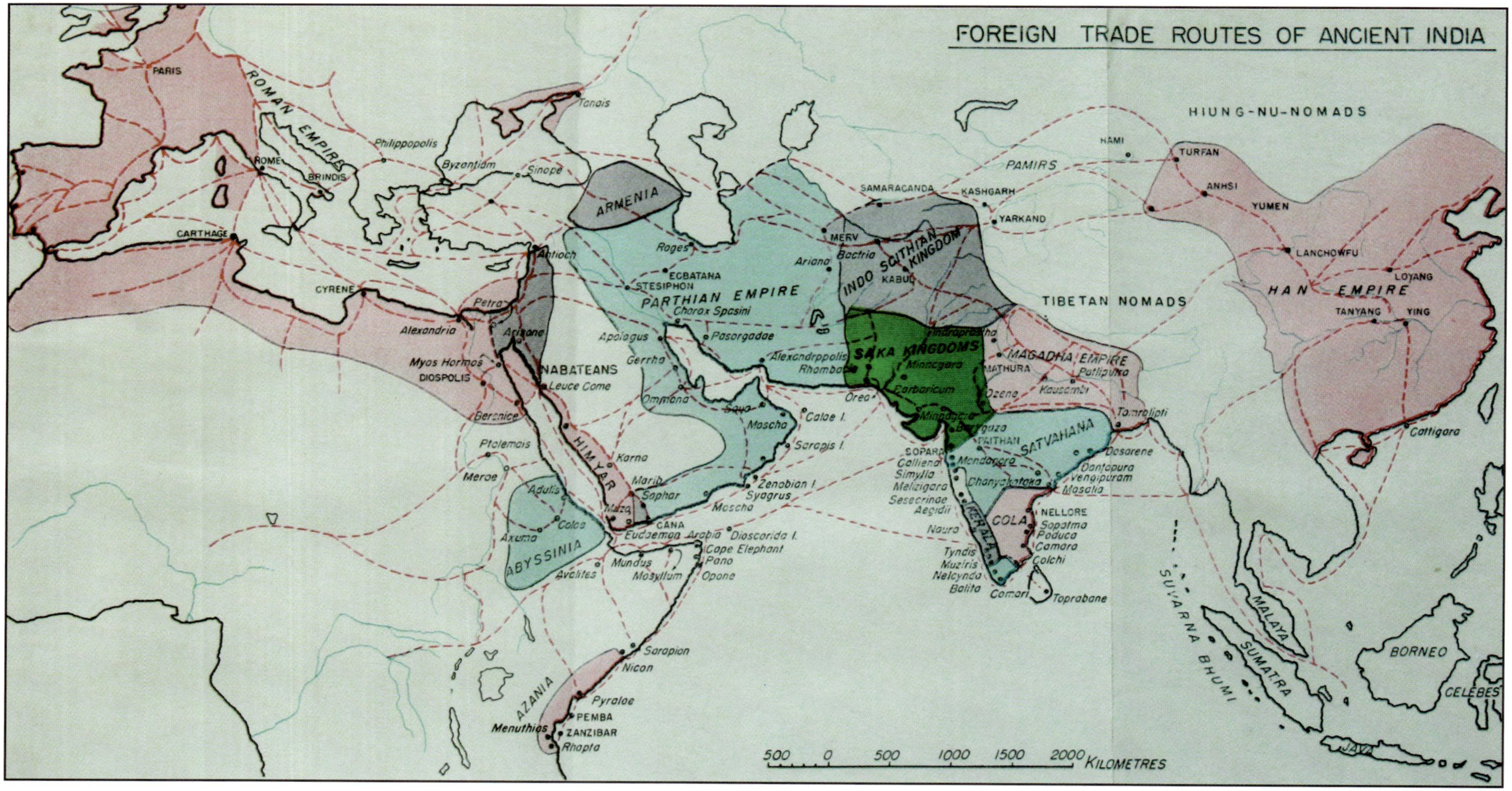

Fig. 3. Foreign trade routes of Ancient India.

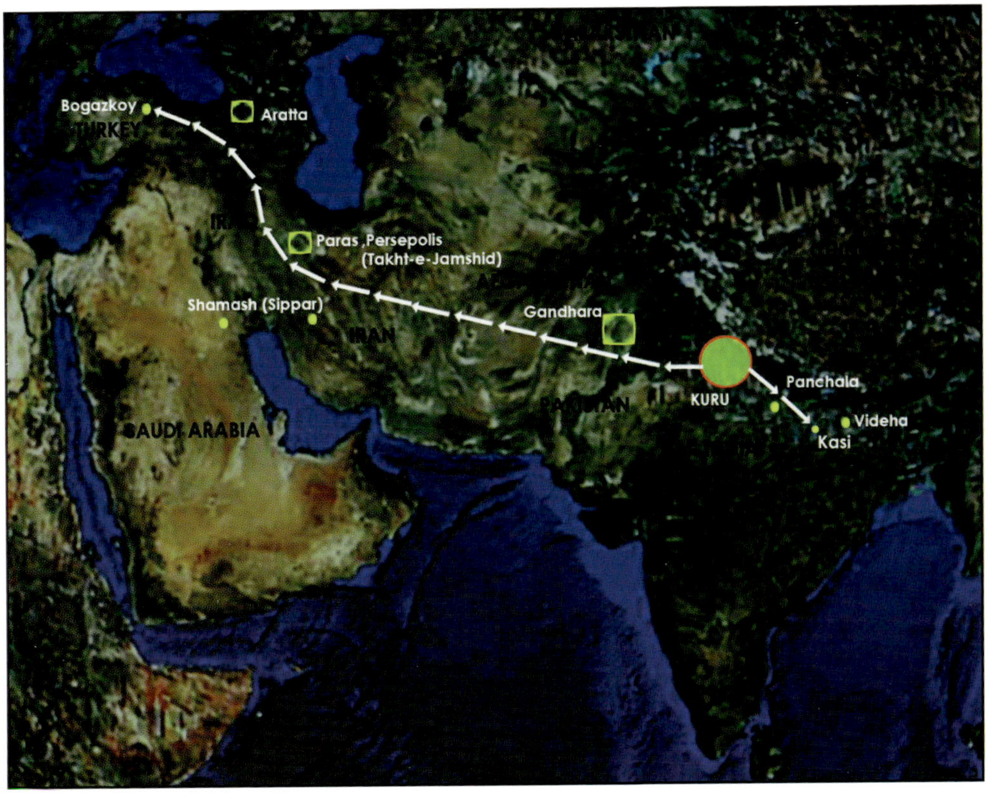

Fig. 4. Migration of people as mentioned in the Baudhayana Srautasutra, a Vedic text.

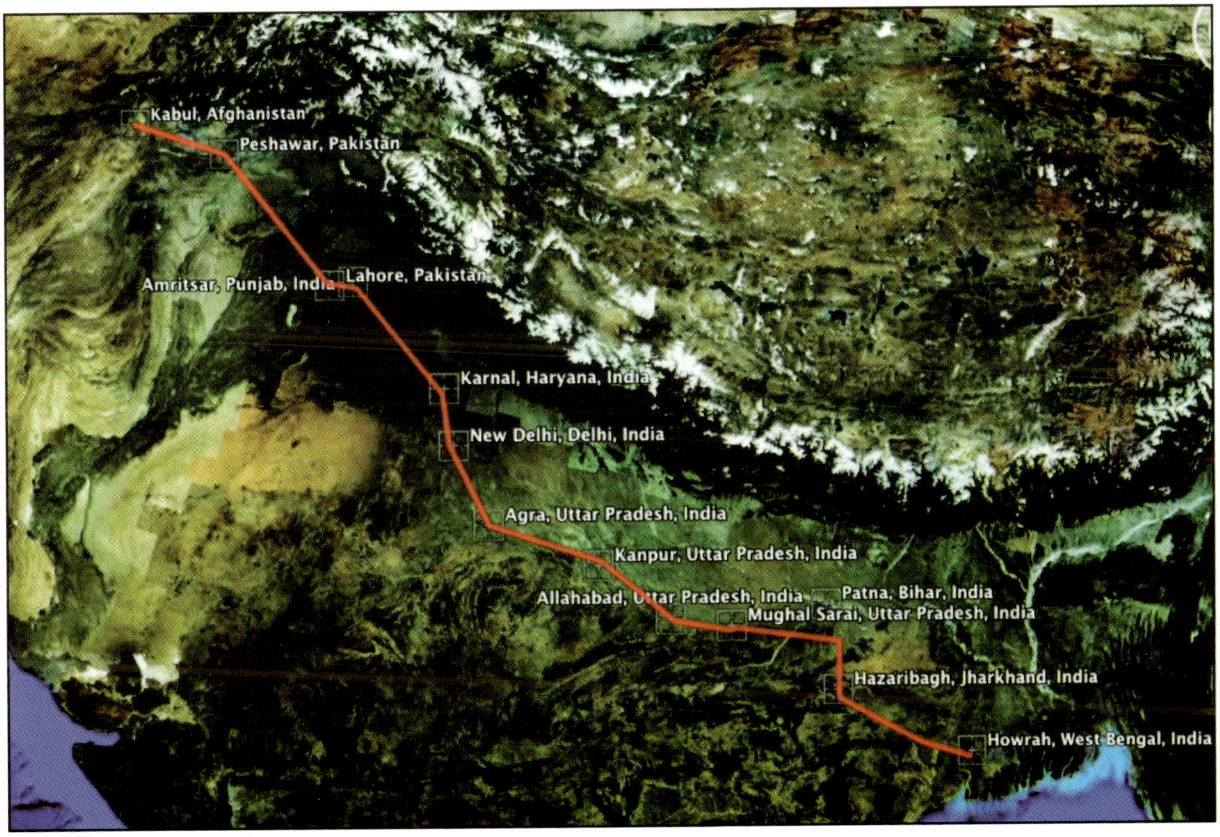

Fig. 5. Road towards Afghanistan in Mauryan era.

... from Agra to Lahor... is all a playne and the highway planted on both sides with trees like a delicate walke; it is one of the great woorks and woonders of the world.

Thomas Roe (1614-18)
Ambassador of James I, the King of England (1603-25), to the Mughal Court

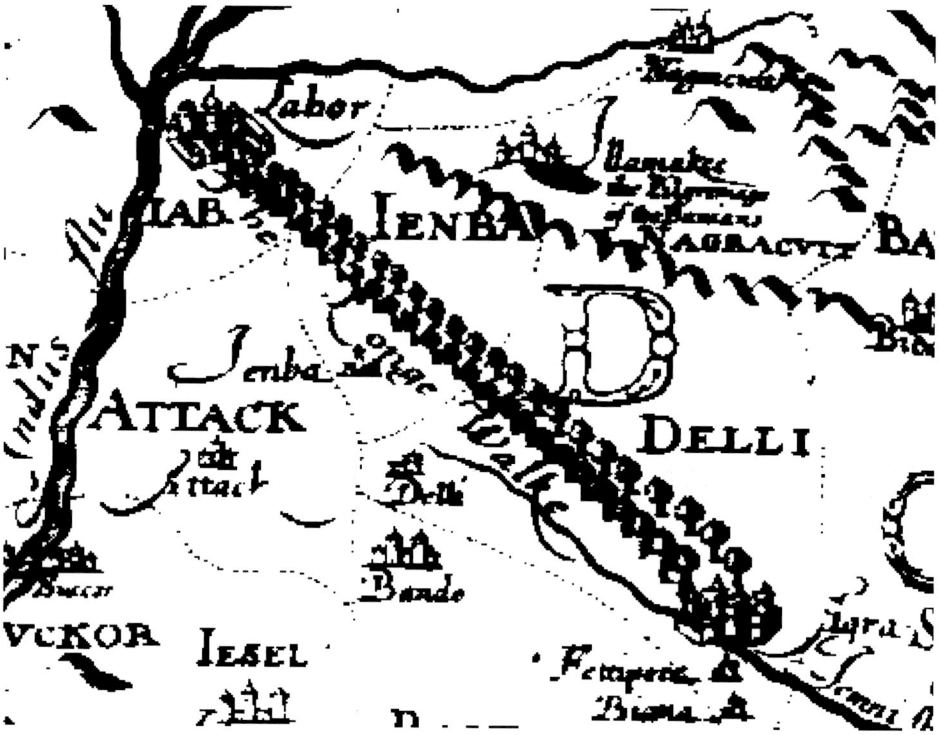

... betwixt Agra and Lahore ... the way is set on both sides with trees.... Every five or six Course, there are Seraes built by the King or some great men, very faire for the beautying the way, memory of their names, and entertainment of Travellers.

Richard Steel & John Crowther
English Visitors to the Punjab (April 1615)

Fig. 6. A drawing by Sir Thomas Roe (1614–18), exhibiting the trees and sarais on the road between Agra and Lahore.

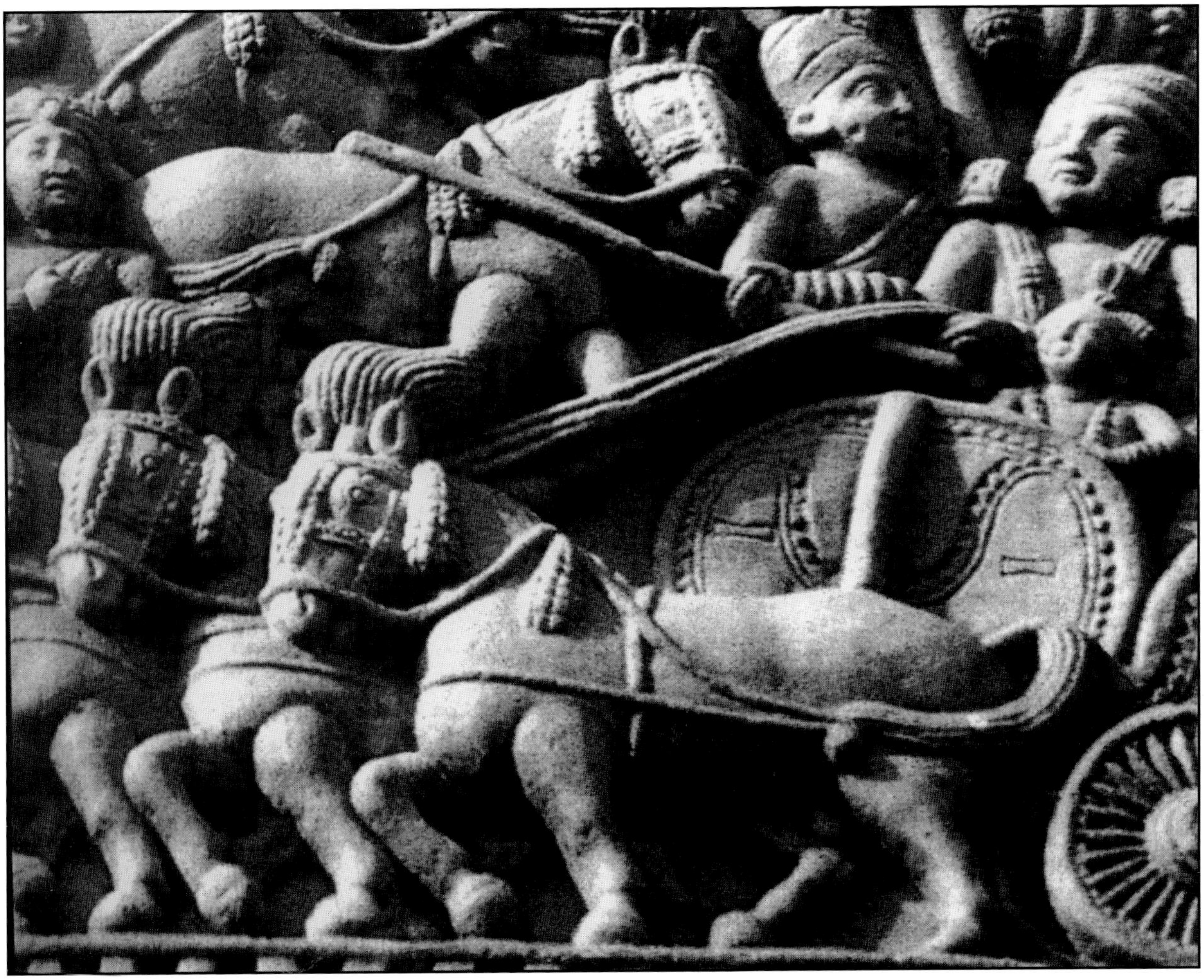

Fig. 7. Relief on the northern gatweway of Sanchi Stupa depicting travel by horse drawn chariot (1st century BC).

responsibility for welfare of the subject. He also deployed soldiers and officers to protect life and property of the travellers and initiated several other righteous deeds as welfare policy.

The Imperial Guptas (4th–6th century AD) held sway over a vast empire after conquering several rulers from north to south and east to west. It was in

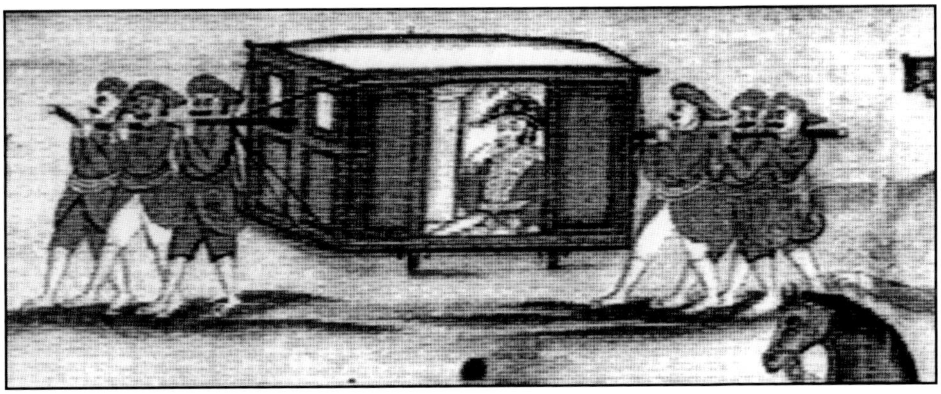

Fig. 8. A painting dated 1820, of the battle of Polilur (1780) showing an European travelling in a palanquin.

pursuance of *Sastric dicta*, and, over and above state policy of *Chakravartin Samrat*. It could only be achieved if vast territories of the empire were well connected and easily accessible with land and river routes. Consequently, it became obligatory state responsibility to maintain and provide adequate infrastructure on ancient routes.

Similarly, in the medieval period Sher Shah Suri (1540–45 AD) adequately consolidated these roads with intention to link together the remote provinces of his vast empire for military and administrative reasons. The *Sadak-e-Azam* (Great Road) as it was then popularly known, has been subsequently recognized as precursor of the Grand Trunk Road. It was soon extended westwards to Multan and eastwards to Sonargaon (now in Bangladesh). The Mughals also consolidated and made it more effectively functional westwards to Kabul in Afghanistan, crossing the Khyber Pass and eastwards to the port city of Chittagong. The early Mughal emperors—Akbar, Jahangir, Shahjahan and Aurangzeb likewise modified it and carried out alterations, additions to infrastructure on these ancient routes. In fact, these routes were the backbone of trade and commerce and effective administrative control over the vast empire

Fig. 9. Historic kos minar in Kanpur.

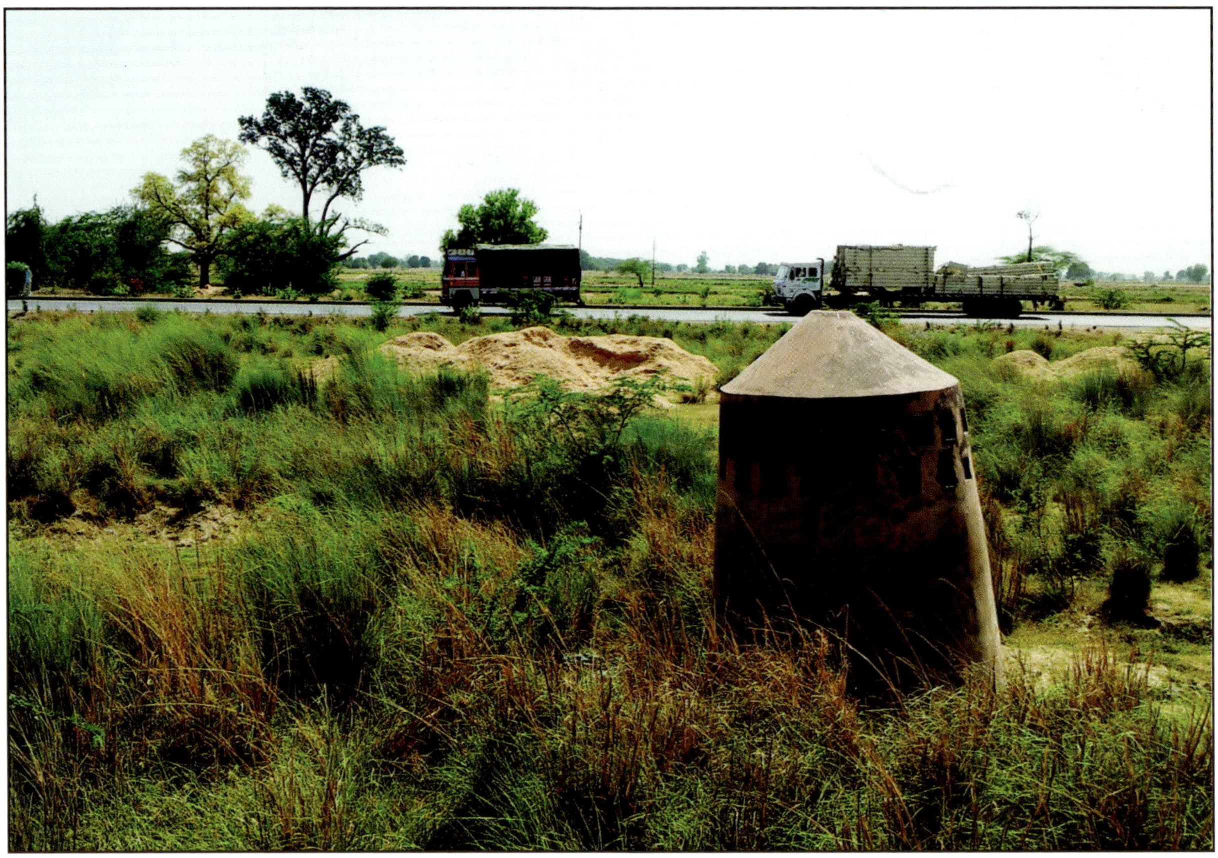

was totally based upon good conditions and regular maintenance of these highways.

The *Sadak-e-Azam* was later improved by the British rulers, and renamed as Grand Trunk Road, extended to run from Kolkata to Peshawar. It was also known as '*Shahrah*'. Of course, it was most significant and well-known route, second only to Trans Asiatic Silk Route.[4] Off and on, it has been mentioned in the literary sources that during ancient and medieval times several roads were covered by thick and dense forest. Even during the Mughal period, vast forest zones posed serious problems to warfare.[5] Groups of traders, and invaders such as Indo-Greeks, Sakas, Kushanas, Hunas, Mongols, and Turks flowed in waves to India through these routes from northwest region for centuries.

A considerable number of edifices serving as integral and essential infrastructure on these routes were constructed from time to time. The noteworthy among them are Kos Minars, *Sarais*, *Dak Chowkies*, Wells, Step-wells, Tanks, *Baolis*, *Pyaus*, Bridges, *Thanas*, *Maqbara* etc. These monuments are of immense archaeological and historical importance and remained in constant use by the travellers. In fact, these monuments are still unveiling contemporary cultural milieu, lifestyle associated with them and signifying glorious past. For elaborate study of trade and trade routes in ancient India (Figs. 2-3), comprehensive documentation of these monuments is essential to understand them in proper perspective from the standpoint of the land, the people and the culture.

Historically speaking, the kos minars are significant archaeological remnants of immense importance and landmark for proper identification of royal routes. The architectural style of kos minars resemble each other except for some minor variations, due to their construction in different periods and phases. One has to keep in mind that during the medieval period the unit of measurement for distance was known as *kos*, which is a corrupt form of Sanskrit word "*krosa*" or Persian word "*kuroh*".[6] The term *kos* remained in use upto recent years even when mile was adopted for measurement of distance. Although, *kos* is now officially replaced by kilometer in modern India but the term is still embedded in the memory of people.

The kos minar literary means a tower (medieval equivalent of a modern milestone) and served as landmark for caravans.[7] Arif *Qandahari writes* "that travelling to and fro goes on day and night and these minars guide them

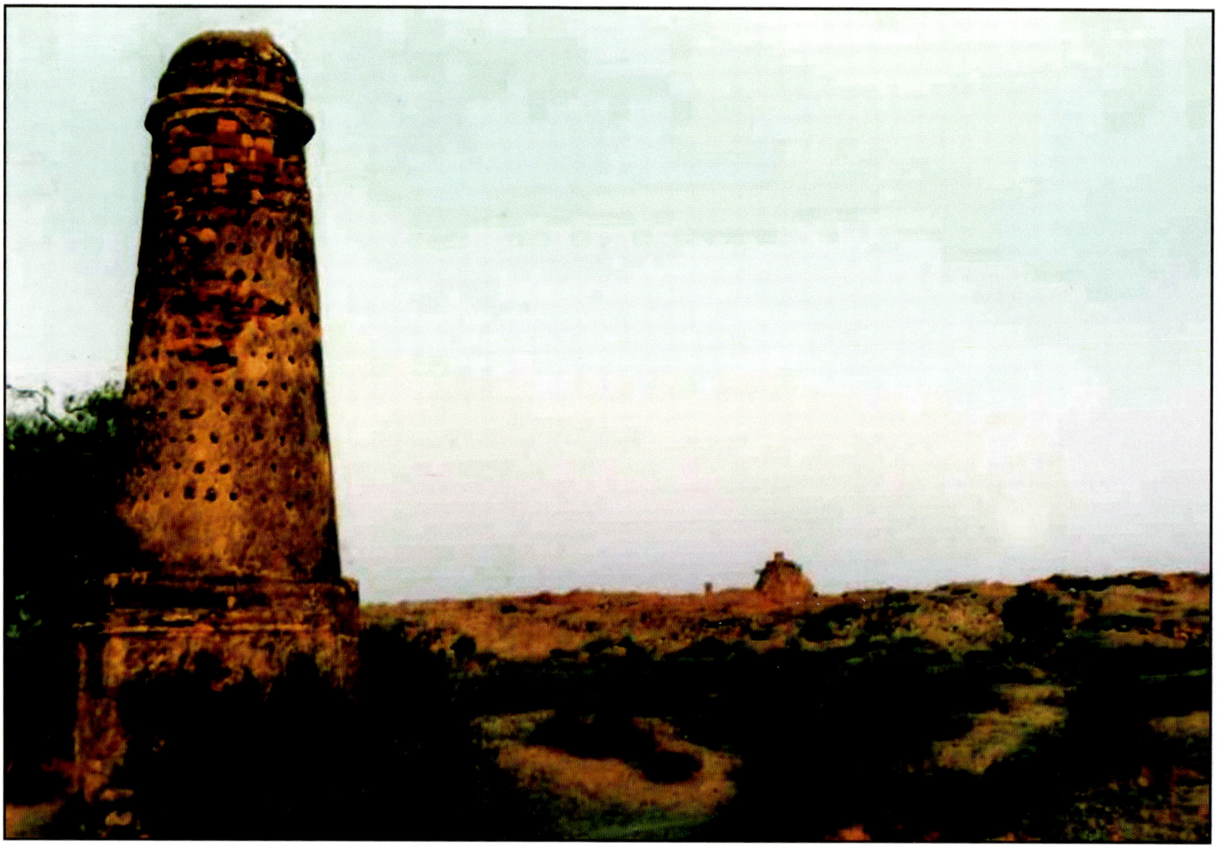

Fig. 10. Kos Minar from Jahangir's period near Ajmeri Gate of Fatehpur Sikri.

Fig. 11. Detail of Jahangiri Kos Minar showing traces of painting.

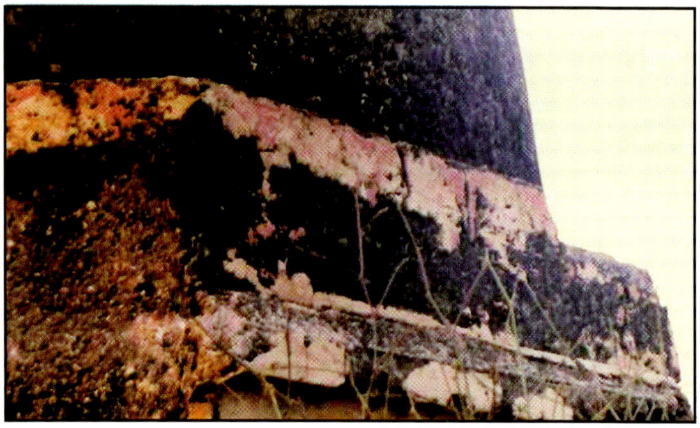

(travellers) from losing their way or getting off the route."[8] Attilio Petruccioli states that "*Kos-minars* which measured the continuous road network established in a theoretically uniform manner throughout the empire starting from the centre also represent a symbolic measurement of territory."[9] Emperor Babur ordered to raise distance-markers each "twelve yards high with a *chardara* on top" at every nine *kos* all along the distance from Agra to Kabul.[10] Akbar also ordered for erection of kos minars along Agra-Ajmer route. Arif *Qandahari* adds that emperor had the horns of deer he killed, affixed to these minars so that each tower was studded with three or four hundred horns. Jahangir ordered the *Faujdar* of Multan that a post be set up every *kos* from Agra to Lahore to show the distance as an act of public welfare.[11]

The architectural style and design of surviving kos minars is basically similar

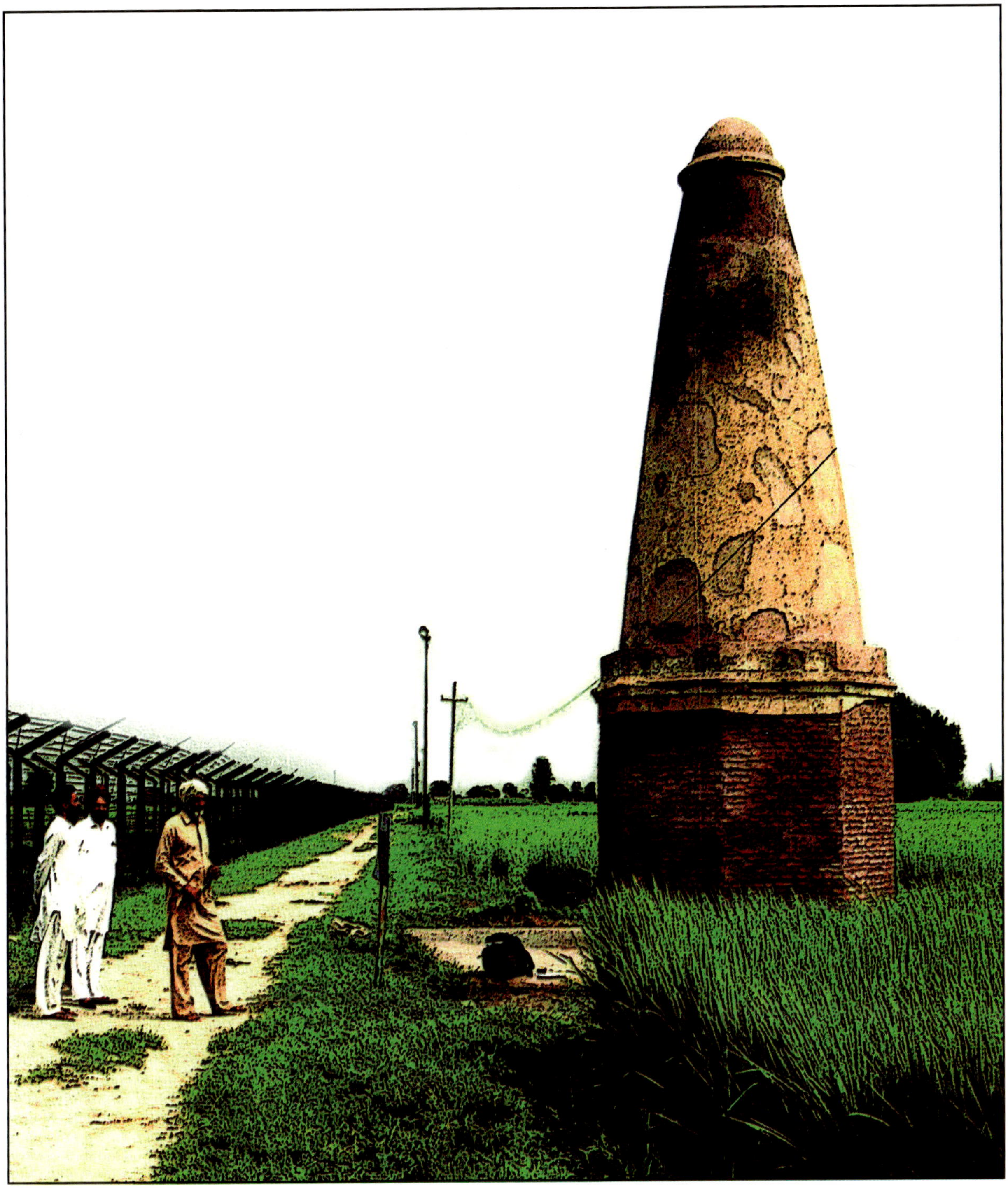

Fig. 12. View of Raja Tal Kos Minar (Jahangir's period) near Indo-Pak Border.

and some of them have graceful proportions, whereas, others are not so. (Figs. 13A-13B) About 30 feet high, these minars were constructed either of bricks or stone rubble masonry and plastered with *chunam* (lime mortar, Figs. 9-12). The kos minars particularly of Jahangir's period bear painting. One such minar

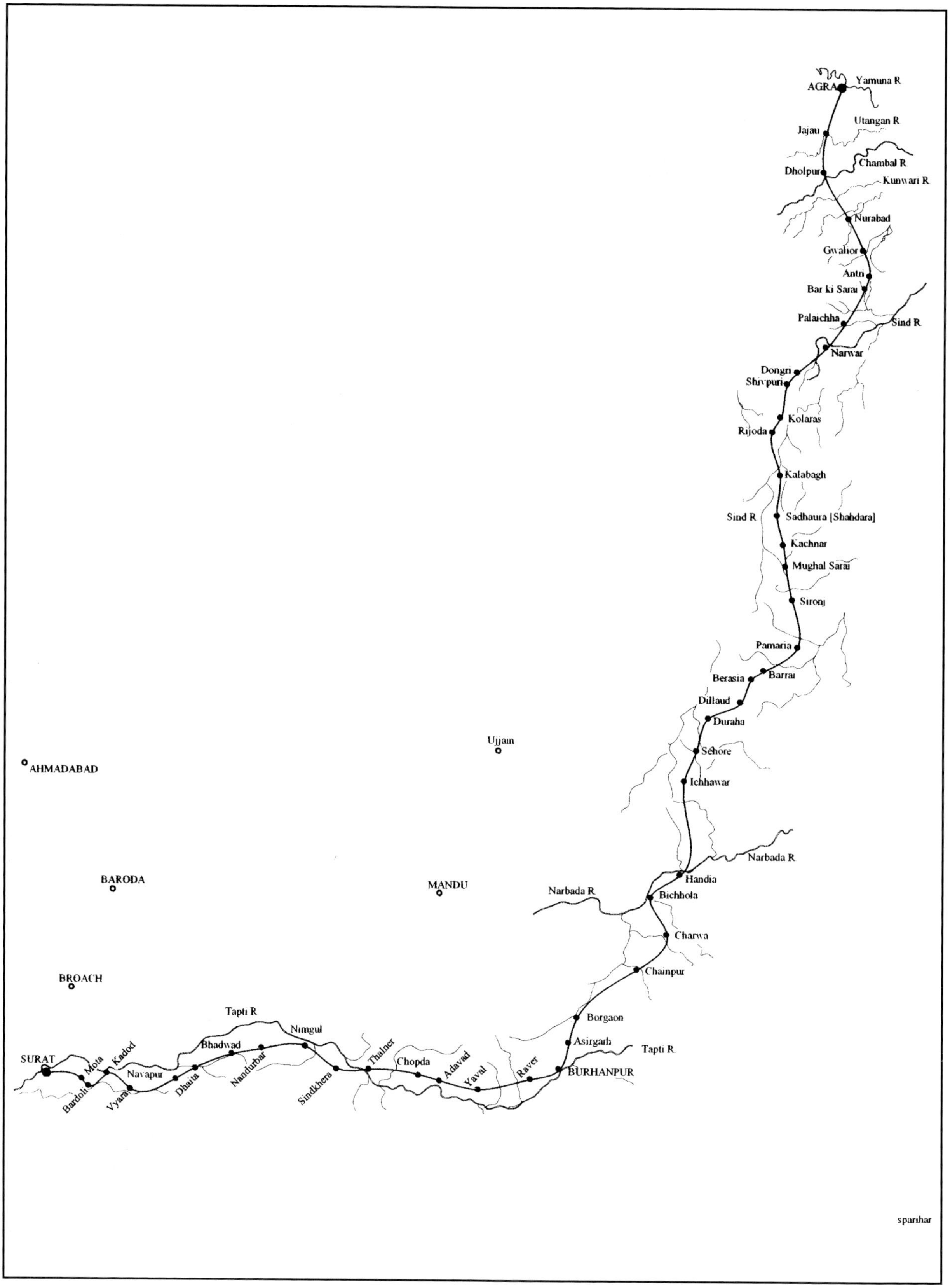

Fig. 13. Ancient route from Agra to Surat through Malwa (after Parihar 2008).

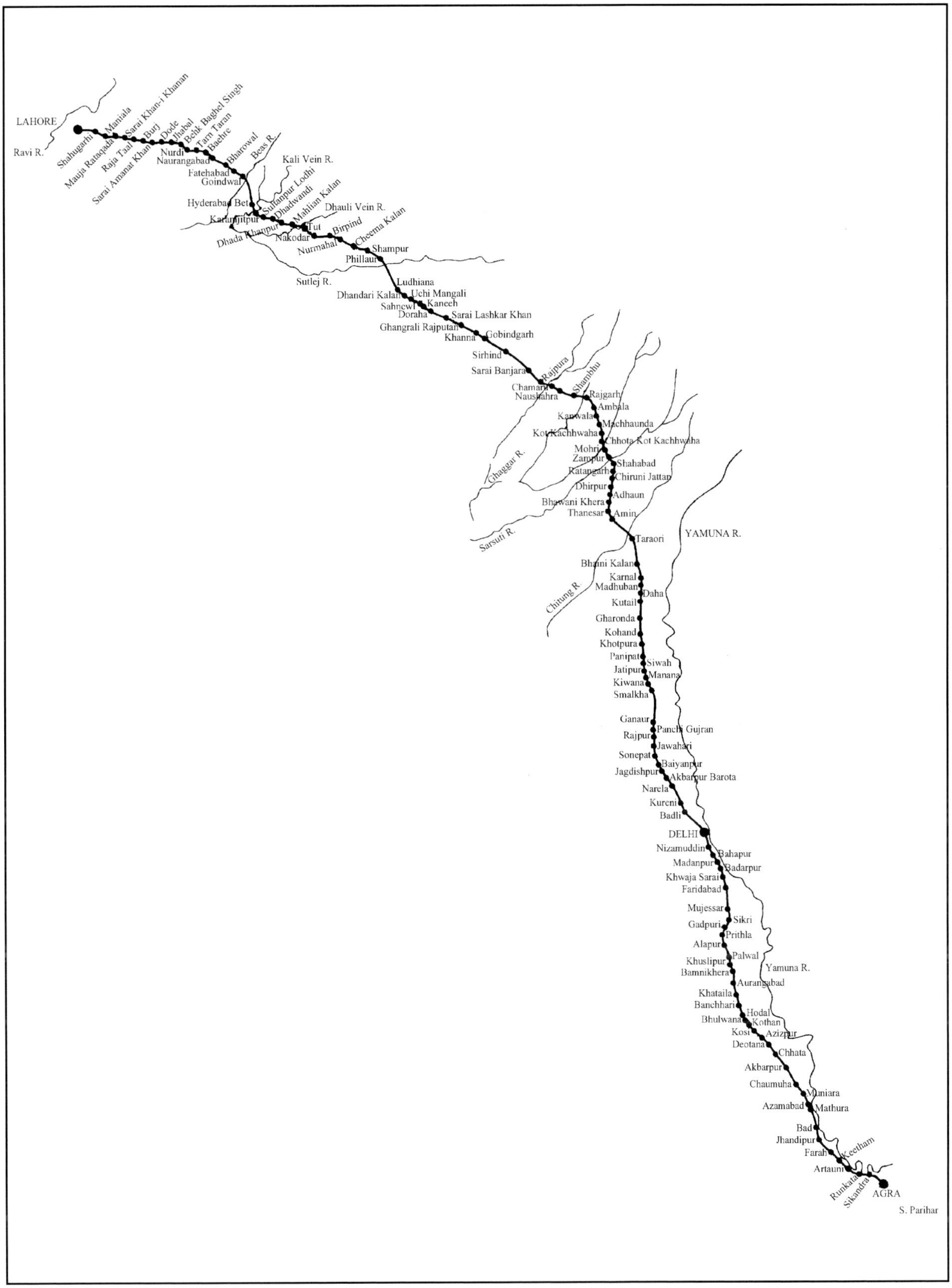

Fig. 14. Ancient route from Agra to Lahore (after Parihar 2008).

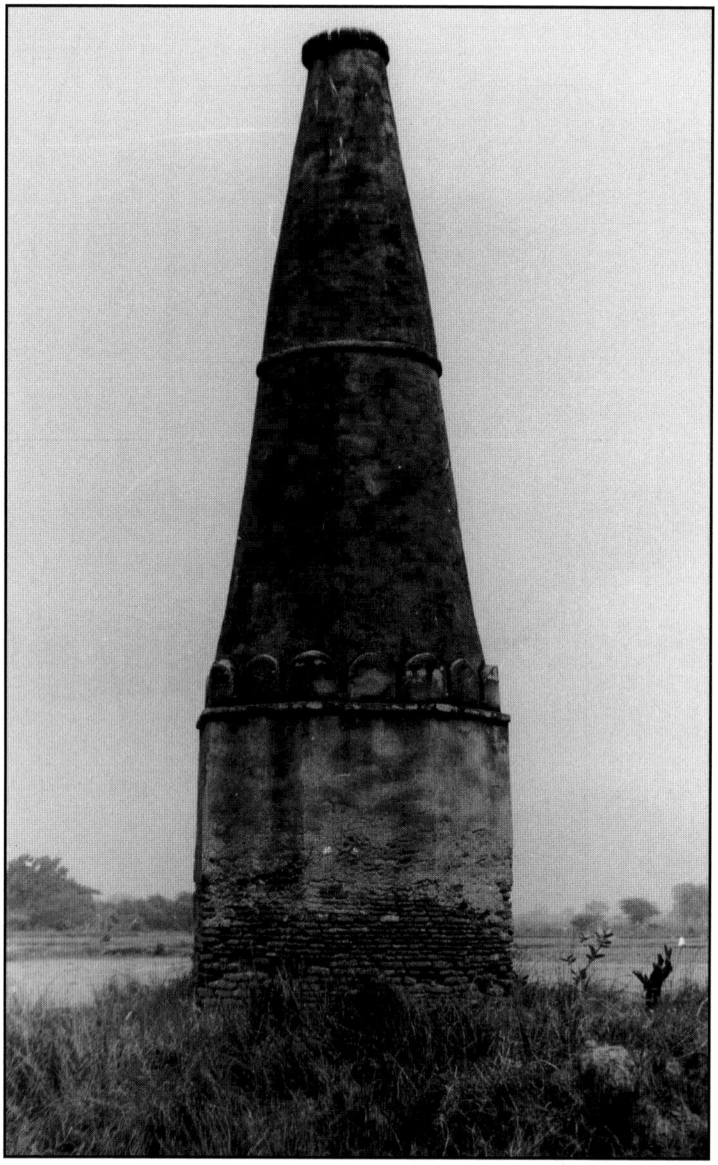

Fig. 15. Chaumuha Kos Minar.

still survives at a distance of 2.5 kos west of Ajmeri Gate, Fatehpur Sikri (Figs. 10-11). Invariably, the kos minars rise from slightly tapering octagonal base, which covers one third of its total height. Therefore, it becomes a tapering cylindrical pillar with circular top. The octagonal base is separated from the central portion by a moulding above which runs a band of moulding or a border of relief, while one more register of moulding is also visible below the spherical top. Rarely, spherical top of a kos minar is found surmounted with architectural member; for example the one at Sikandara has a crowning finial.[12] But, it appears to be wrong conservation carried out by Conservation Assistant without application of architectural sense. On the basis of research conducted by Sir Sayyid Ahmad Khan on kos minar, he mentions that each minar originally bore the serial number of the kos.[13] It appears that in due course of time above stated stones could not survive and have never been found fixed in situ on any kos minar. It is also mention worthy that during course of survey conducted by us, no evidence or impression of such stone slab on any kos minar has ever been found or noticed.

The kos minars were erected on the royal route from Agra to Ajmer via Jaipur in west, from Agra to Lahore via Delhi in the north and from Agra to Mandu via Shivpuri in south (Figs. 13-14). On either side of these highways, kos minars are found alternately standing at a distance of two and a half miles (equivalent to one Shahjahani *kos*). In Mughal period, *mewras* (*pyada*) and horses were deployed on these highways with assigned duties to deliver royal messages/*farmans* and *dak* as soon as possible.

Even at far away distances from the capital, proper arrangements for exchange of horses, round the clock deployment of *dak* officials at respective duty places was ensured for speedy delivery of royal communications and personal secret messages. This system was under the control of a separate administrative head, *Daroga-e-Dak-e-Kul Mumalik-e-Mahrusa*.

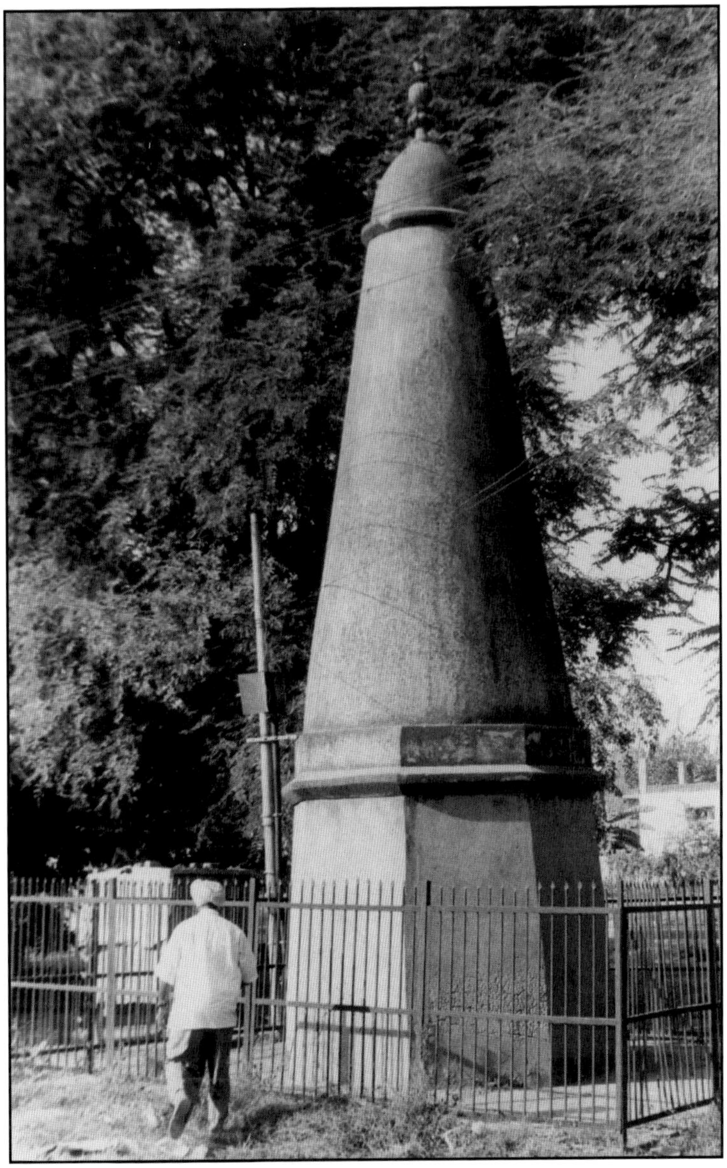

Fig. 16. Kos Minar at Sikandara.

The field survey and research on the subject have revealed that surviving kos minars are of three varieties. The above observation is based on architectural style, availability of adjoining facilities for travellers and their geographical location. The archaeological remains found in situ and literary references on the subject further corroborate the above observation. The three categories are as follows:

(a) Architecturally simple and ordinary kos minars without supplementary infrastructure and traveller's facility available nearby. Such minars were erected basically for landmark identification exclusively.

(b) Kos Minars depicting contemporary architectural features/style and attributed with provisions of limited traveller's facility.

(c) Exemplary kos minars having sufficient infrastructures (*Sarai*, *Baoli*, Well, Mosque, *Idgah*, *Thana*, *Pya-u*, *Dak-chowki* etc.) and all possible traveller's facilities with ensured arrangement of safety and security.

Keeping in view the above classification, several kos minars situated along the road between Agra, Fatehpur Sikri and Ajmer, and, from Delhi up to Lahore fall under the first category. For example, kos minars located at Sikandra, Chaumuha, Chhata, Artauni, Keetham, Bad (Agra), Muniara, Akbarpur, (12 kos from Bad), Deotana (6 km before Kosi), Azizpur, Kosi (103 km before Delhi), Kotban (8 km before Hodal) (Dist. Mathura), Bhulwana (4 km before Hodal) (Dist. Faridabad), Banchari (Dist. Faridabad), Khataila (17 km before Palwal), Aurangabad (13 km before Palwal), Khuslipur/Khusropur (4 km before Palwal), Alapur (5 km past Palwal), Prithla (15 km before Ballabhgarh), Miranpur (13 km after Palwal), Sikri (6 km before Ballabhgarh) (Dist. Faridabad), Badarpur, Madanpur (near Apollo Hospital, New Delhi), Zoological Park (New Delhi), Pipalthala (Delhi), Kureni (near village Bhorgarh), Narela (near railway line, Delhi), Akbarpur Barota (Sonepat), Jagdishpur (Sonepat), Baiyanpur (Sonepat), Jawahari and Rajpur (Sonepat), Panchi (near Larsauli, Sonepat), Ganaur (Sonepat), Smalkha (Panipat), Kiwana (near village Jurasi, Panipat), Manana (Panipat), Jatipur (Panipat), Siwah (near Dullapur, Panipat), Khotpura (Karnal), Kohand (Karnal), Karnal (near Transport Nagar), Taraori (Karnal), Thanesar (Kurukshetra), Zainpur (Kurukshetra), Mohri (before the village between NH-1 and railway line), Chhotakot Kachhwaha (Ambala), Kanwala (Ambala), Rajgarh (Patiala), Chamaru (Patiala), Ghungrali Rajputan (Ludhiana), Sahnewal (Ludhiana), Shampur (Jalandhar), Nakodar (Jalandhar), Sultanpur Lodhi (Kapurthala), Tarantarn (Amritsar), Kanpur Dehat, (Kanpur) etc. are noteworthy under this category. (Figs. 15-17).

Fig. 17. Chhata Kos Minar.

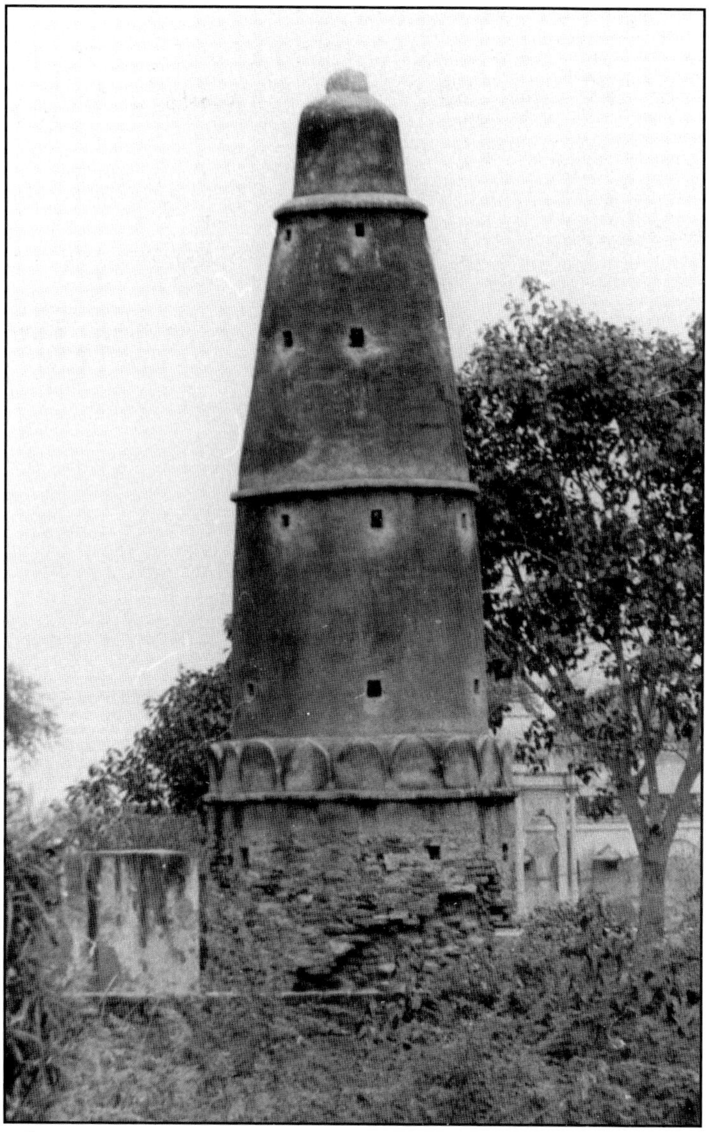

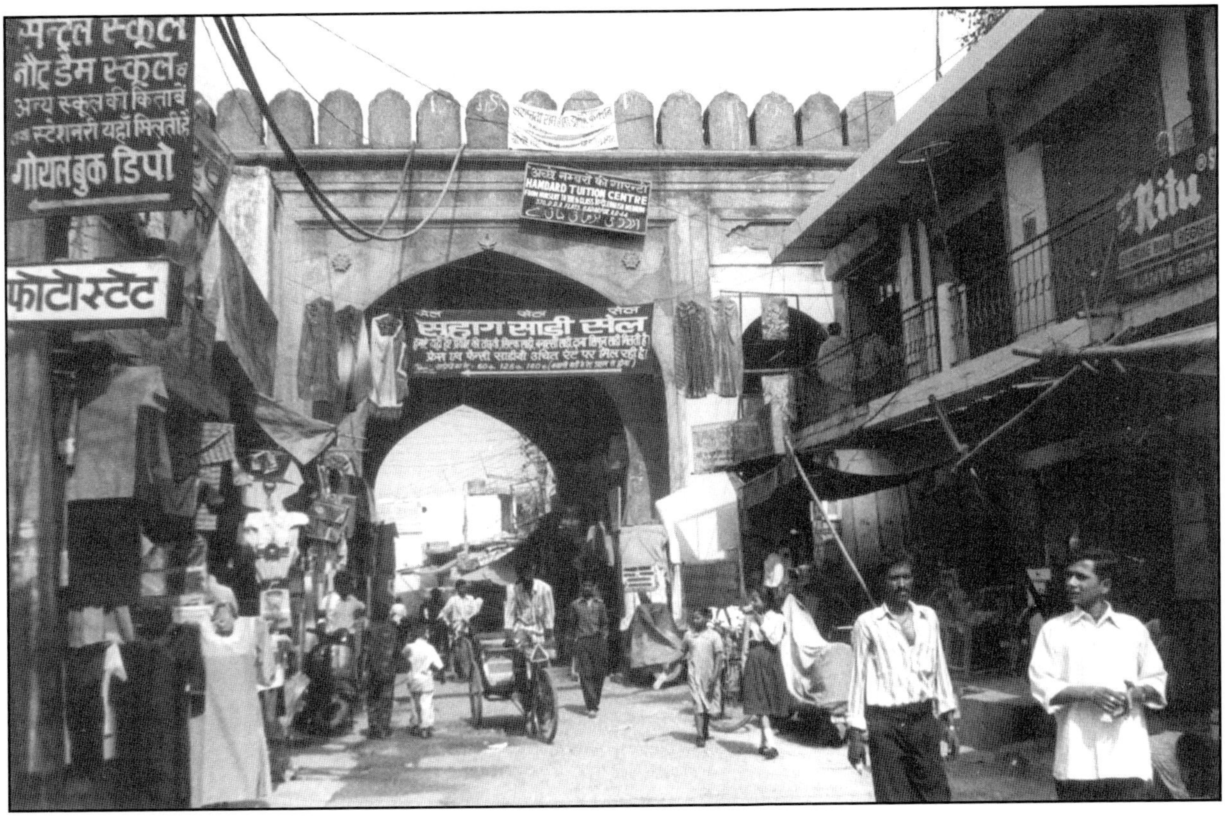

Fig. 18. Badarpur Sarai.

Badarpur Sarai (Badarpur) kos minar falls under the second category of kos minars, which has limited traveller's facilities like sarai, well, mosque, market etc. (Fig. 18).

The third category of kos minars is represented by Hiran Minar of Fatehpur Sikri, Chor Minar in Hauz Khas, New Delhi and Neem Sarai Minar in Malda district of West Bengal. Location wise, these minars are significant and architecturally appear to be unique as well as of immense historical importance. These kos minars with adjoining infrastructures have all possible traveller's facilities, safety and comfort, basically required during long tiring journey.

Architecturally, the minars of this category (Hiran Minar, Chor Minar and Neem Sarai Minar) have close resemblance with each other so far as their style, shape and location is concerned. Fortunately, above minars have still survived, more or less in their original condition or partly damaged. However, nomenclature such as Hiran, Chor and Neem Sarai are misnomers and definitely are later attribution with them. These monuments derived above cited names subsequently.

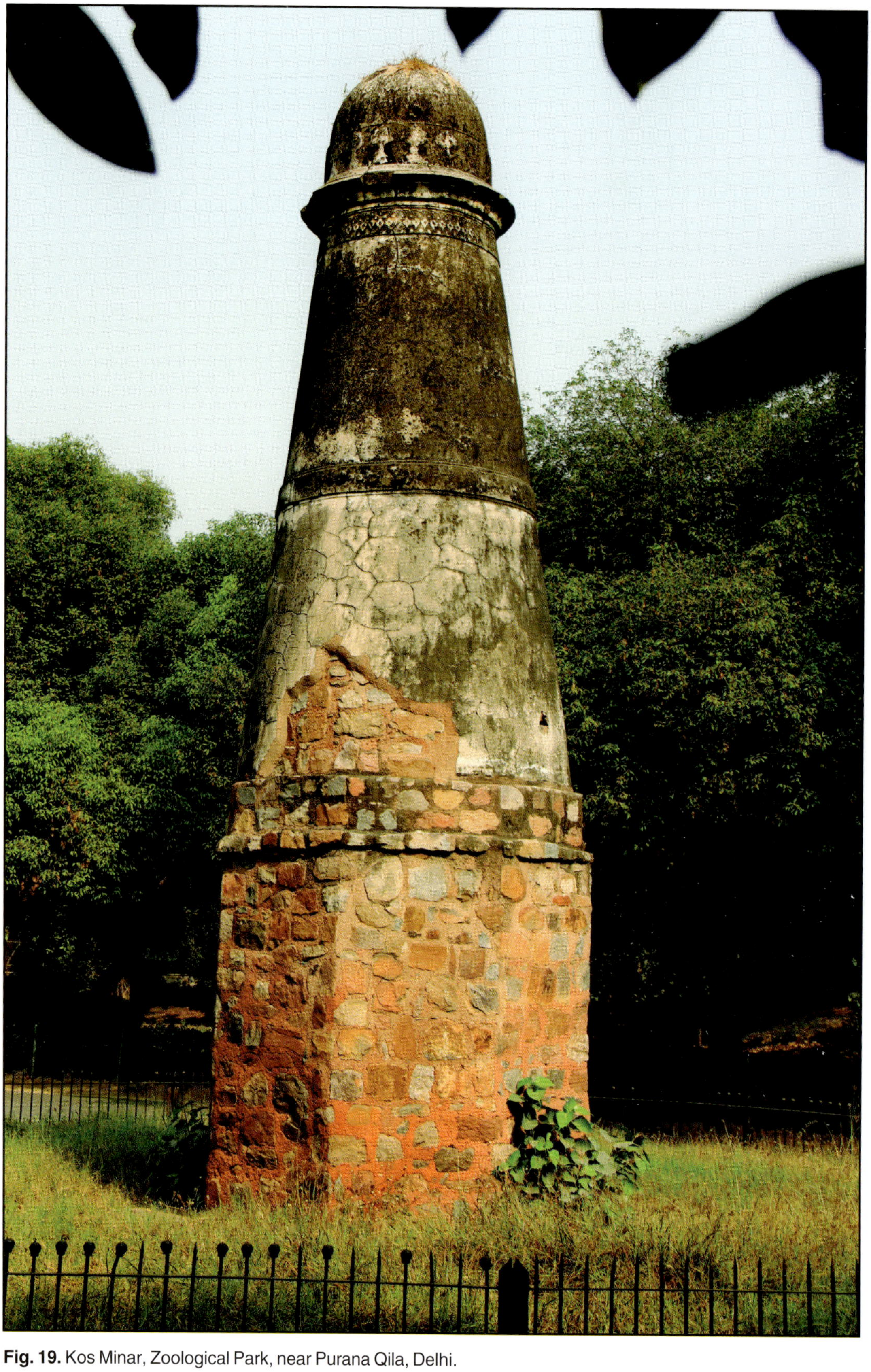

Fig. 19. Kos Minar, Zoological Park, near Purana Qila, Delhi.

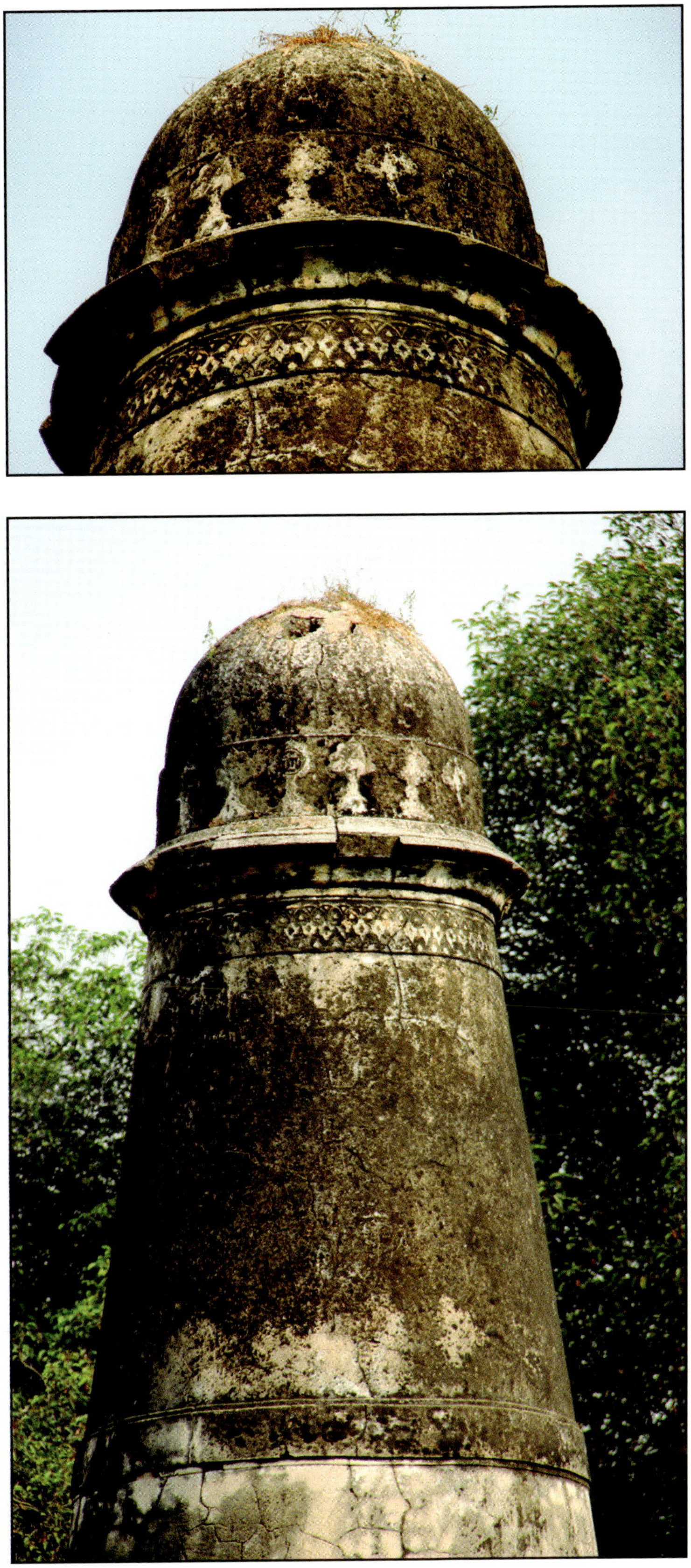

Fig. 20. Kos Minar, Zoological Park, near Purana Qila, Delhi (details).

References

1. Subhash Parihar, *Land Transport in Mughal India*. New Delhi, 2008, p.3.
2. Ervad M.F. Kanga and N.S. Sontakke (ed.), *Avesta Part III Vendidad and Fragments*. Poona, 1978, pp.2-3.
3. B.B. Lal, *The Homeland of the Aryans: Evidence of Rigvedic Flora & Fauna and Archaeology*. New Delhi, 2005, p.88.
4. Subhash Parihar, *op. cit.*, p.5.
5. *Ibid.*
6. *Ibid.*, p.13.
7. *Ibid.*, p.89
8. *Ibid.*
9. *Ibid.*
10. *Ibid.*
11. *Ibid.*
12. *Ibid.*, p.90.
13. *Ibid.*

2 Hiran Minar

The Hiran Minar (Lat.27°05′55" N; Long.77°39′45" E), constructed in 16th century, is located in front of Hathi Pole. It is about 22 m high and stands on an octagonal platform which itself rests on a square platform (Fig. 21). The tower is octagonal up to the height of about four metres and circular for the remaining height (Fig. 22). The circular part of the tower is decorated with stone replica of elephant teeth. On the top, it is surmounted with a *chhatri*. The tower is entered through a flat topped door and provided with spiral staircases. The most distinguished feature associated with the minar is the water management system.

There is a curious water system at the Hiran Minar. On its back, towards the lake, is a small well (*kui*) (Fig. 23). Water was drawn from the well and passed by monolithic *nalis* (channels) under the floor of the plinth (*chabutara*) through a monolithic inlet almost at the middle of its height (Fig. 24). Thence water flowed underground presumably through similar stone *nalis*, to the other side of the plinth, where at the exact corner; it fell down through a stone gargoyle-mouth. It has been completely defaced, but most probably it was (fish) *makara*-shaped (Fig. 25). Water was collected in a tank which has now been completely renovated.[1]

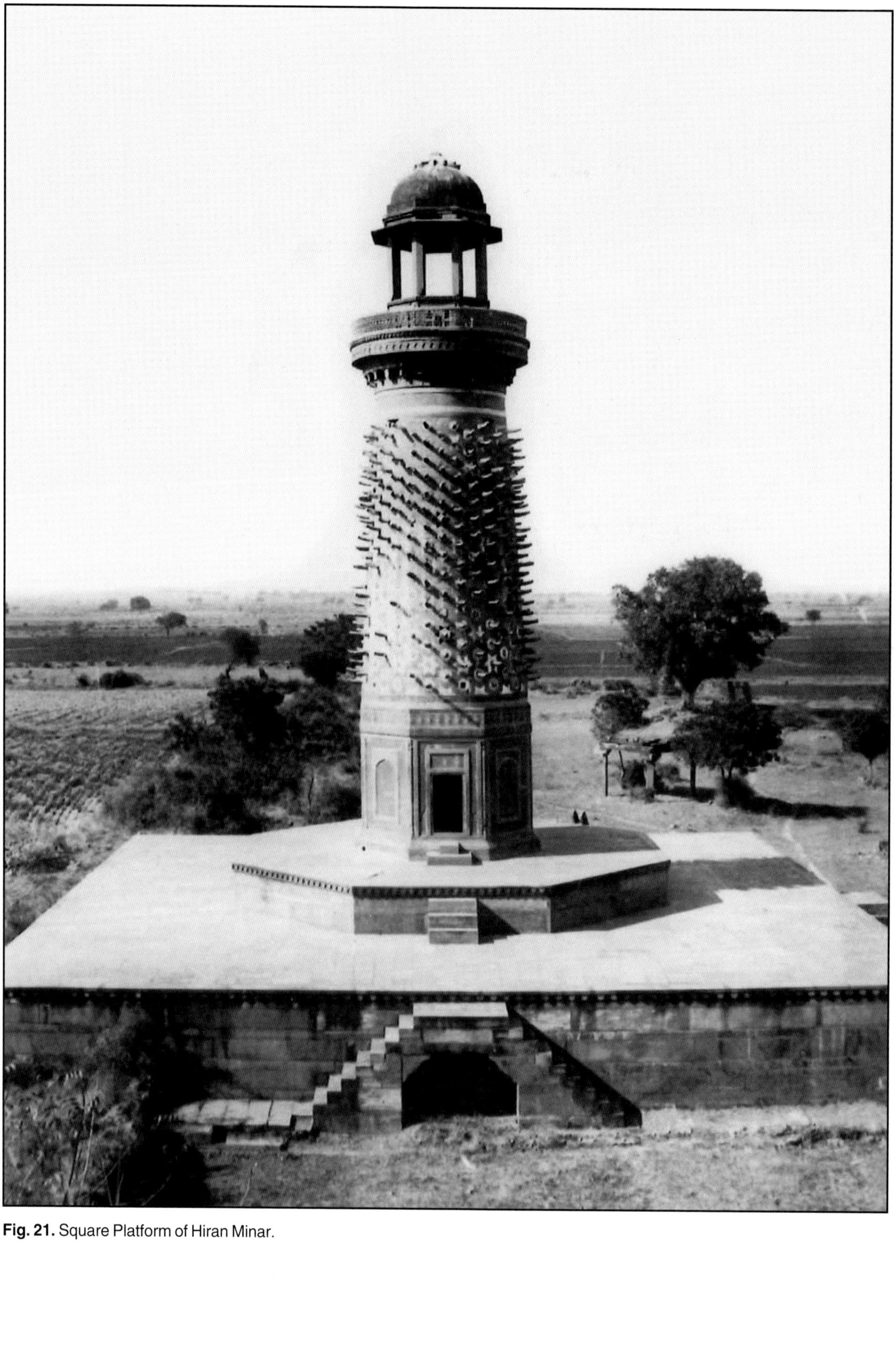

Fig. 21. Square Platform of Hiran Minar.

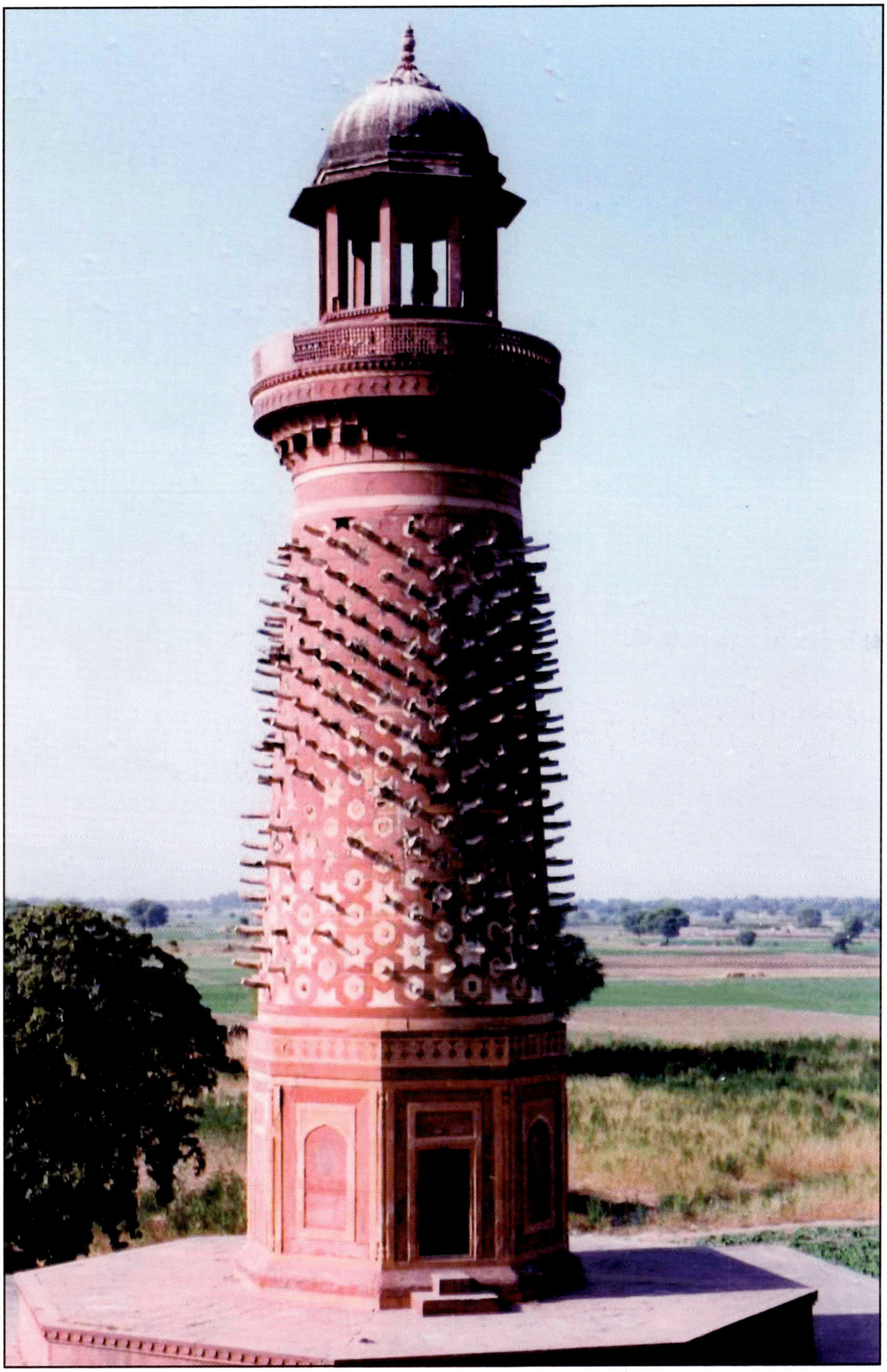

Fig. 22. Hiran Minar: architectural form.

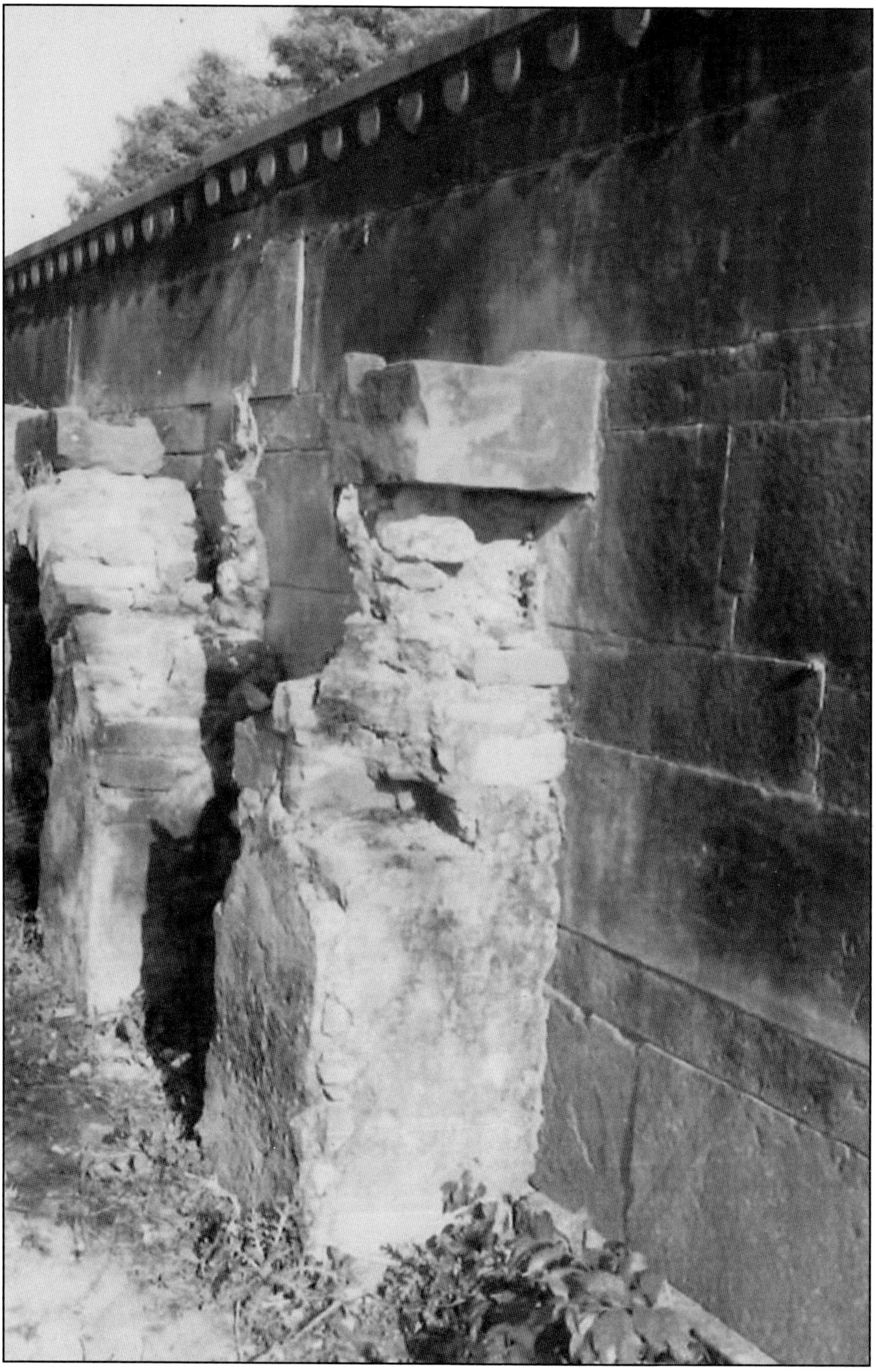

Fig. 23. Nali along the platform of Hiran Minar.

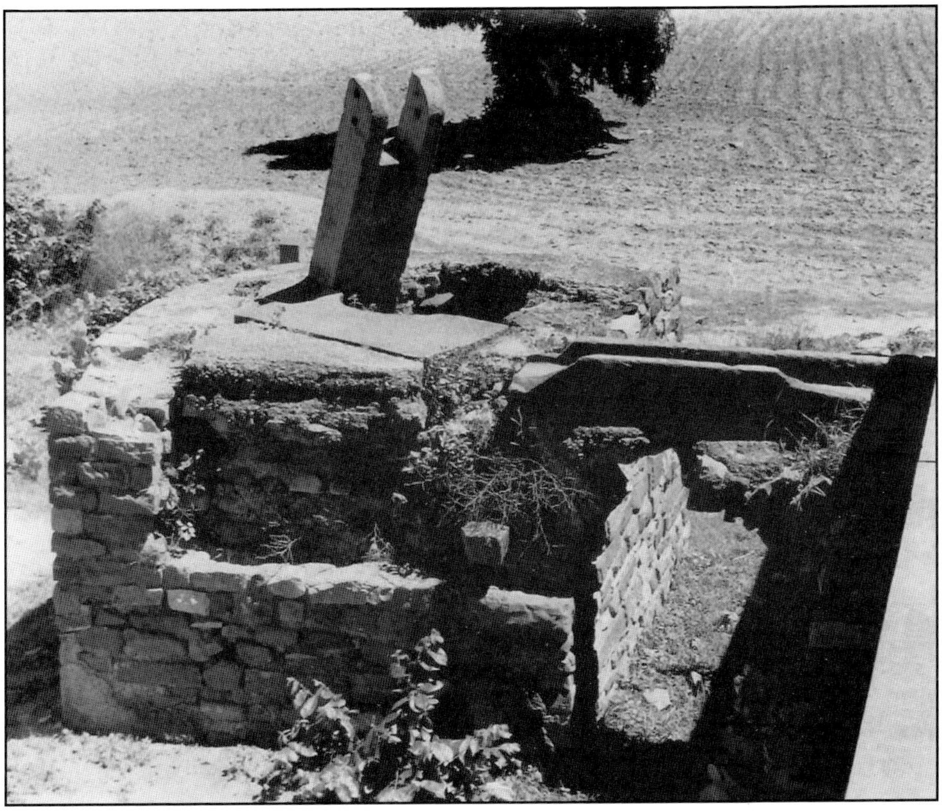

Fig. 24. Kui abutting Hiran Minar.

This simple system ensured the provision of water both for man and cattle at the Hiran Minar which was the first kos minar at Fatehpur Sikri. It was an integral part of the institution of imperial roads-and-sarais and it was incumbent

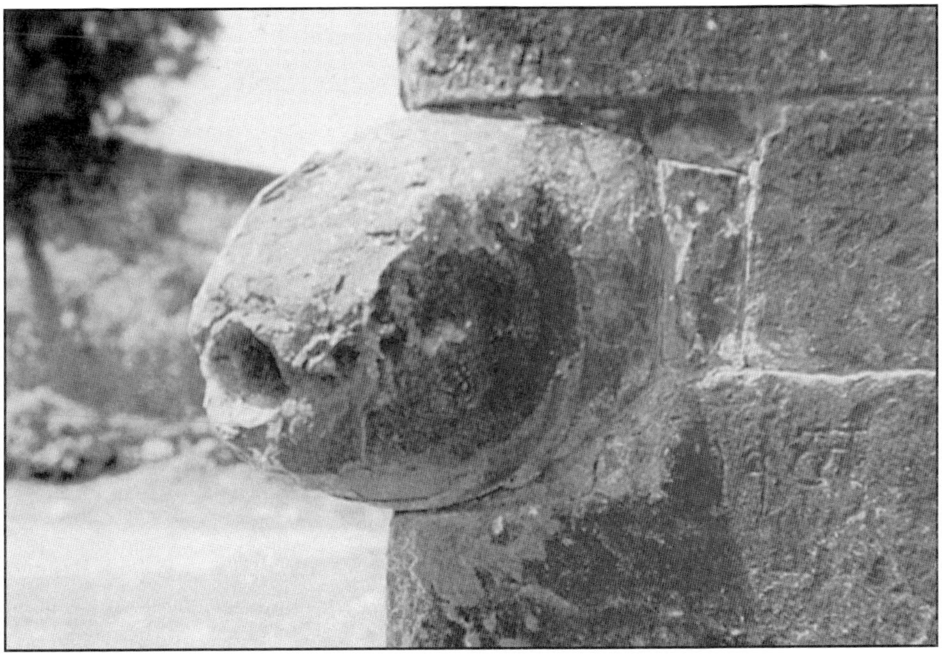

Fig. 25. Fish-shaped water outlet.

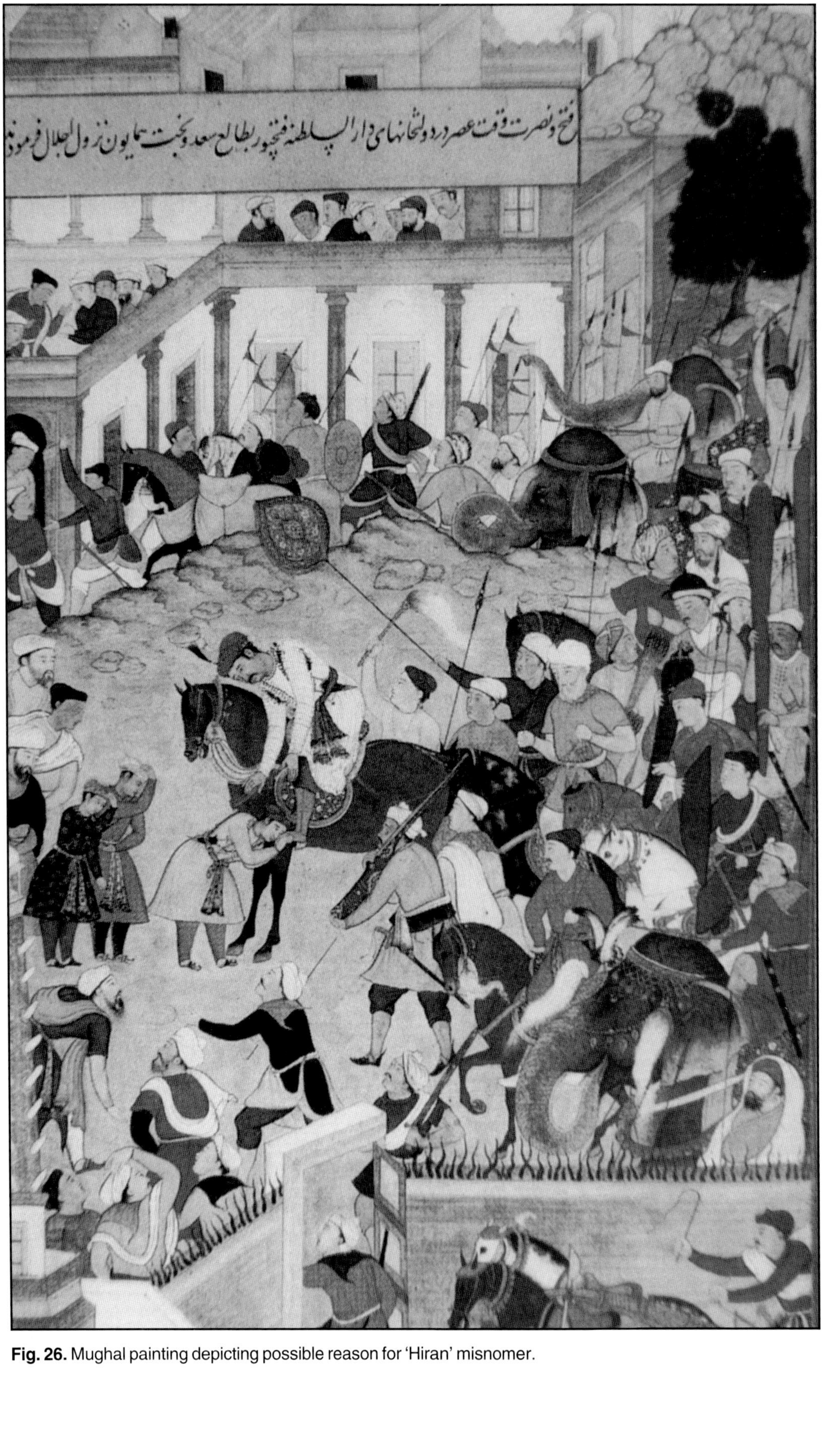

Fig. 26. Mughal painting depicting possible reason for 'Hiran' misnomer.

to build a well, step-well, tank or *pya-u* (*sabil*, water-hut) with a kos minar for the convenience of the travellers. This system was also founded at great expense, being underground for the provision of a constant water-head at this point where the travellers either ended or began their journey.

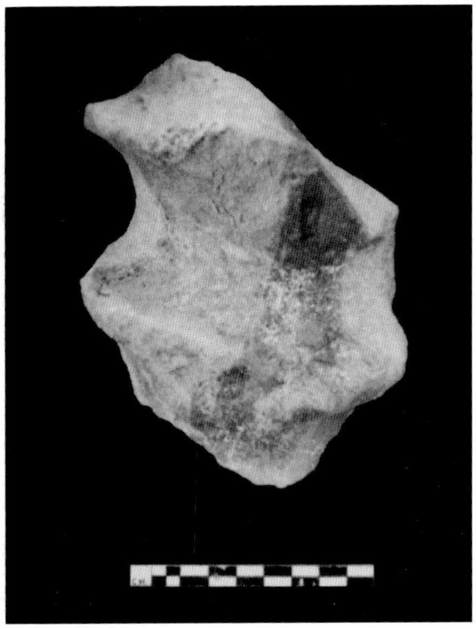

In this context reference is cited of a Mughal painting (Fig. 26). It depicts boldly serial blackbuck horns, embedded firmly and fixed on enclosure wall of '*Hiran-Bara*' which was built by Emperor Jahangir near so-called Hiran Minar. The Minar is also distinctly visible on bottom-left portion in this painting. It seems that Hiran Minar derived the present nomenclature, consequently, due to its situation in the vicinity of '*Hiran-Bara*'. This fact has further been confirmed with the discovery of a broken blackbuck horn of stone found near Hiran Minar during exploration (Fig. 27). It suggests that buildings were also located originally in front of Hathi-Pol, and on the lake-side also which gradually collapsed. The location of *caravansarai* adjoining Hathi-Pole (Fig. 28), further without any ambiguity

Fig. 27. Broken blackbuck horn of stone found near Hiran Minar.

Fig. 28. Sarai adjacent to Hiran Minar.

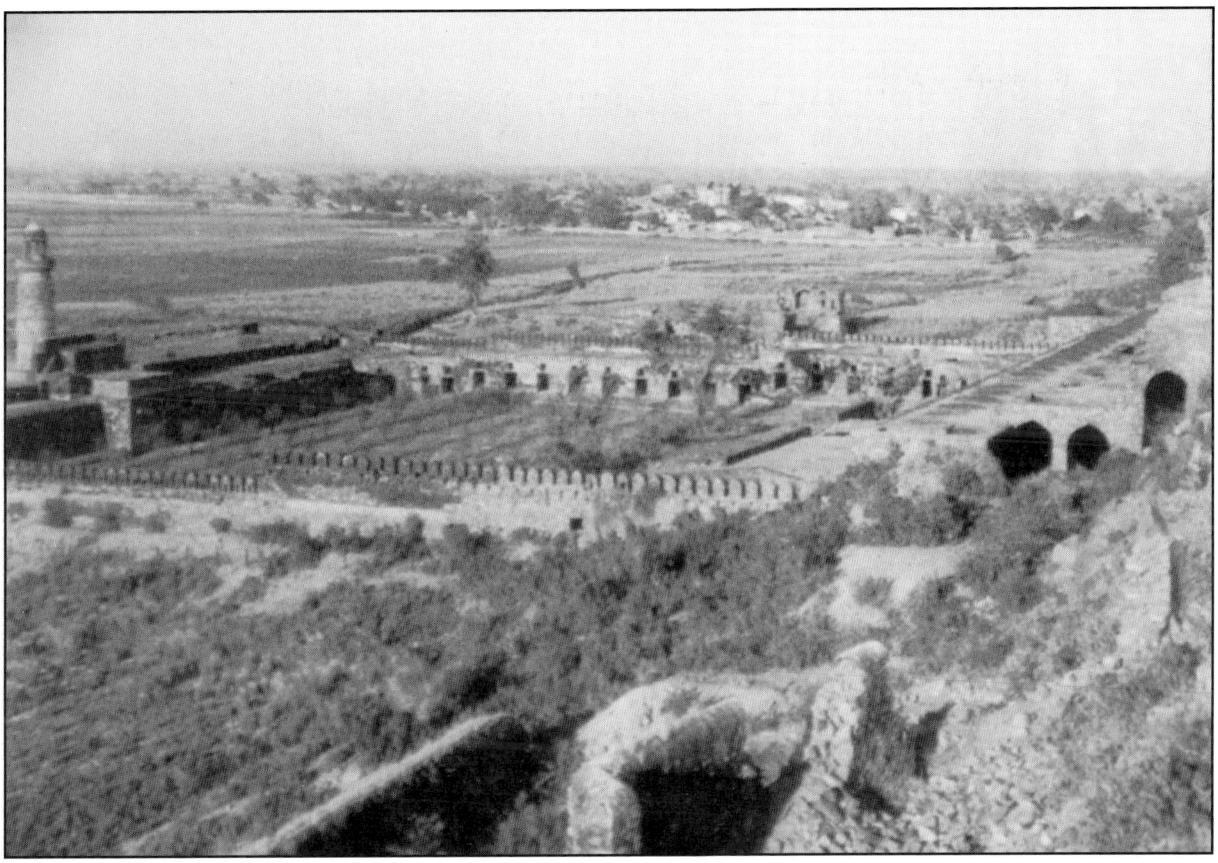

suggests that it was also an integral part of the communication system and essential facility for comfort of travellers.[2]

References

1. D.V. Sharma, *Archaeology of Fatehpur Sikri: New Discoveries*. New Delhi, 2008, pp.94-95.
2. *Ibid.*

3 Neem Sarai Minar

Another minar known as Neem Sarai Minar (Lat.25°01'25" N; Long. 88°07'52" E) is equally of immense historical importance and is architecturally akin to Hiran Minar. The Neem Sarai Minar constructed in 16th century is located in Malda district of West Bengal, half way between Gaur and Pandua, and, has been erected at the confluence of two rivers, namely *Kalindri* and *Mahananda*.[1] The minar stands on octagonal base having arched interior cells (Fig. 29). The upper part of the minar is broken and pierced with holes and embedded stone replicas of elephant's teeth externally. It is provided with entrance gate and steps leading to the top which was probably surmounted with a cupola. Due to its location outside the ancient city, on the river bank, it appears that prime function of this minar was to guide river route traders and travellers.

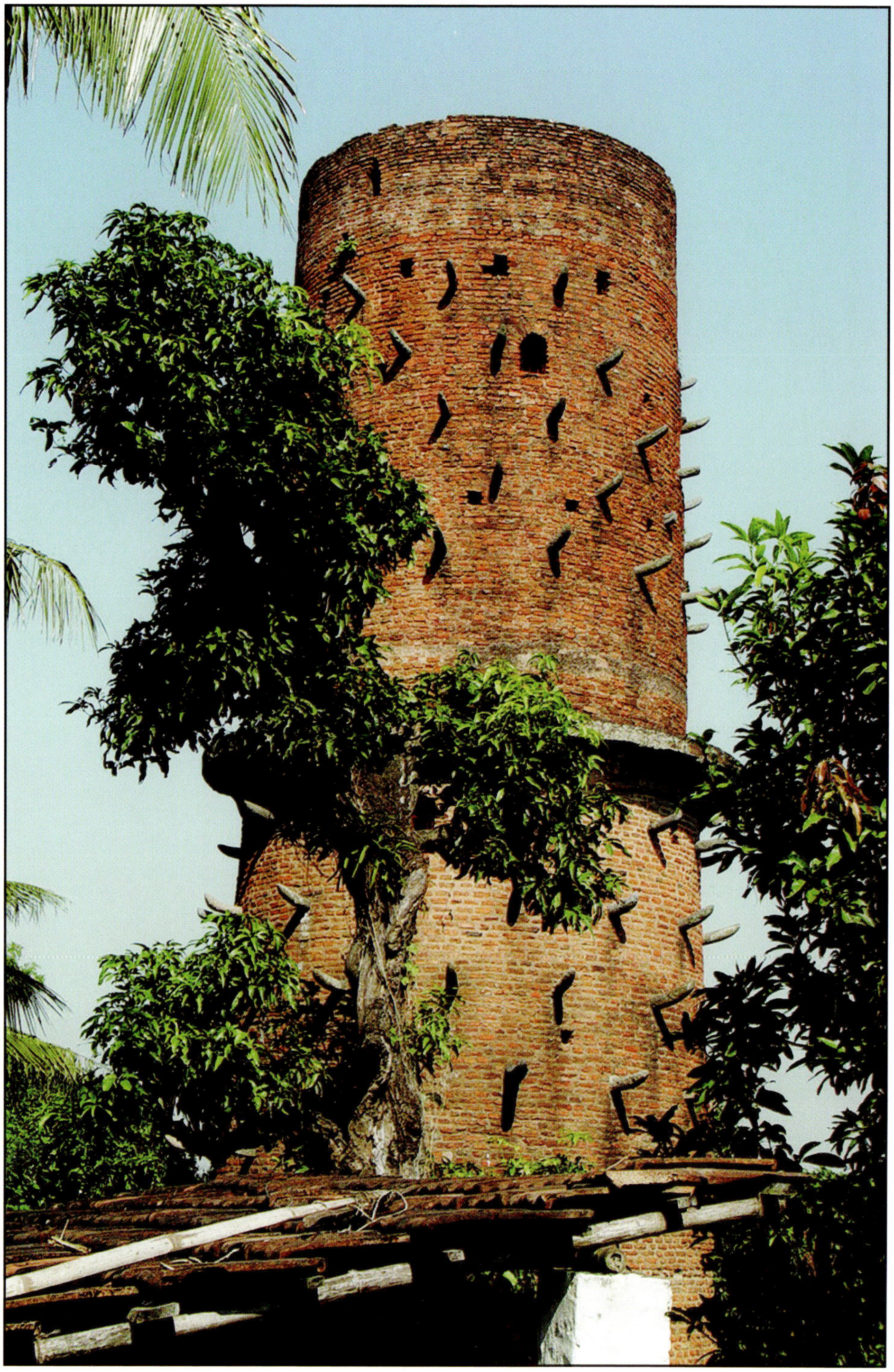

Fig. 29. Neem Sarai Minar at Malda.

References

1. Abid Ali Khan, *Memoirs of Gaur and Pandua.* 1986.

4 Chor Minar

The third important minar is Chor Minar (Lat. 28°32'5"; Long. 77°39'45"E), which to some extent is architecturally comparable to Hiran Minar and Neem Sarai Minar (Fig. 30). It is situated in Hauz Khas Enclave area roughly 100 metres south-east of *Idgah*. It has been declared as Centrally Protected Monument by ASI, vide Gazette notification no. 4700-Education dated Delhi, the 19th August, 1924 comprising of area 900 square feet bounded by Khasra No. 353 north, Khasra No. 353 south, Khasra No. 353 east, Khasra No. 353 west respectively. Name, description and number of the monument (in the revenue boundary of Kharera Village) are given as Chor Minar No. 289[1] by Maulvi Zafar Hasan, Assistant Superintendent, Archaeological Survey of India, who had been specially deputed for listing purpose under J.A. Page and J.F. Blakiston, Superintendent, Archaeological Survey of India, in the then Northern Circle, Agra, for Muhammedan and British Monuments (March 23, 1920).

It is rubble masonry built tapering tower rising from a square (9.20 m) platform, endowed with three arches on each side (Fig. 31-32). The central arch of eastern side has entrance and is provided with a spiral staircase in its interior having a total of 33 steps (Fig. 33). The upper part of the minar has been broken and its available height upto the platform is 8.30m. The total

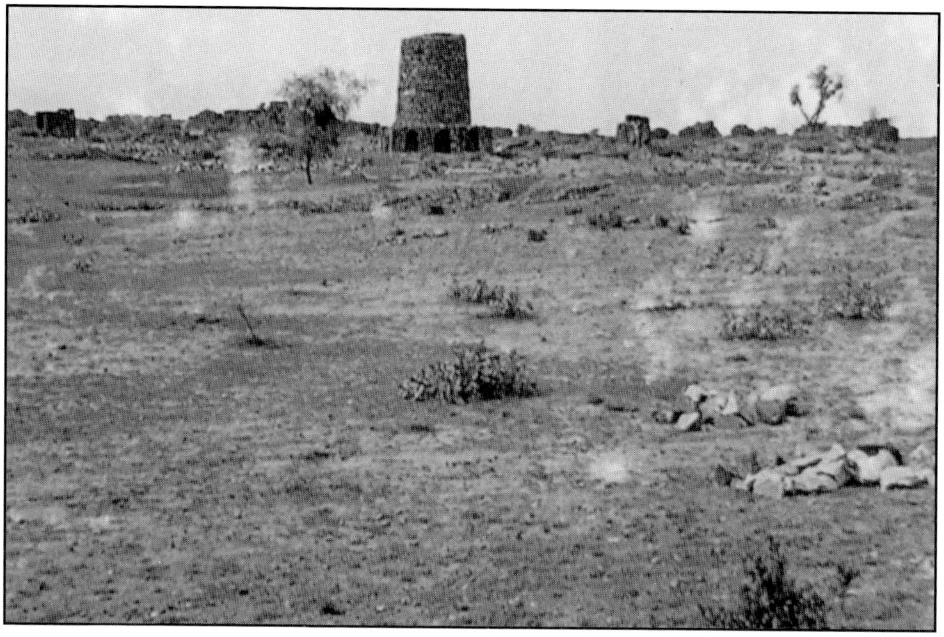

Fig. 30. An archival photograph of Chor Minar.

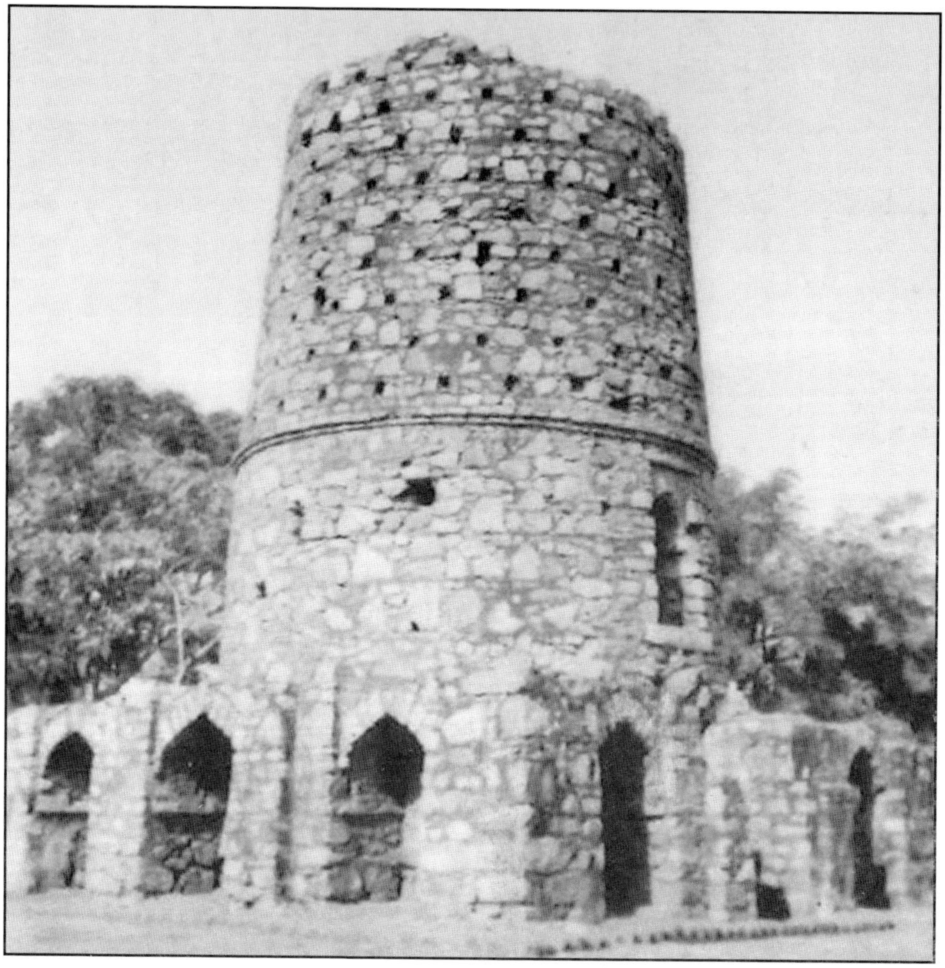

Fig. 31. An archival photograph of Chor Minar.

height including the platform is 10.55 m. On its exterior, several circular holes (now 204 holes are existing) of unascertained use are visible upto the height of 5m from the top (Fig. 34). The southern, western and northern side of the minar are provided with oblong shaped ventilation while the eastern side has an arch shaped opening for adequate light and air (Fig. 35).

Like Hiran Minar, it also appears to be an important kos minar constructed along the ancient highway, in front of western gateway of Siri, the capital city, founded by Ala-ud-Din Khilji, about the year 1303 AD. It is believed by some scholars that heads of thieves (*chor*), who were caught and beheaded, used to be placed in these holes to deter others from engaging in theft and highway robbery. This is how it derived its name as Chor Minar. The proportions of the structure and existing staircase leading upwards certainly confirms original existence of some super structure over it (Fig. 36). The same has probably collapsed in due course of time. Akin to Hiran Minar, in fair amount of certainty, some stone architectural members were perhaps originally fixed externally in above holes which disappeared subsequently.

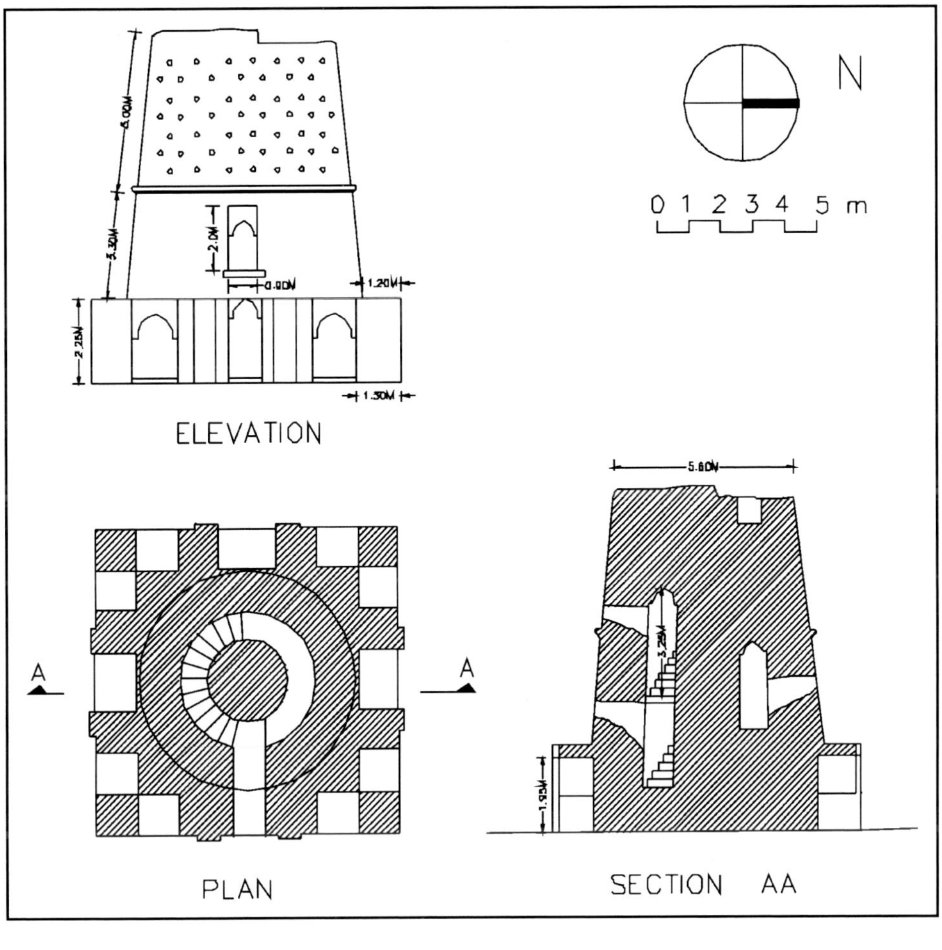

Fig. 32. Architectural documentation of Chor Minar.

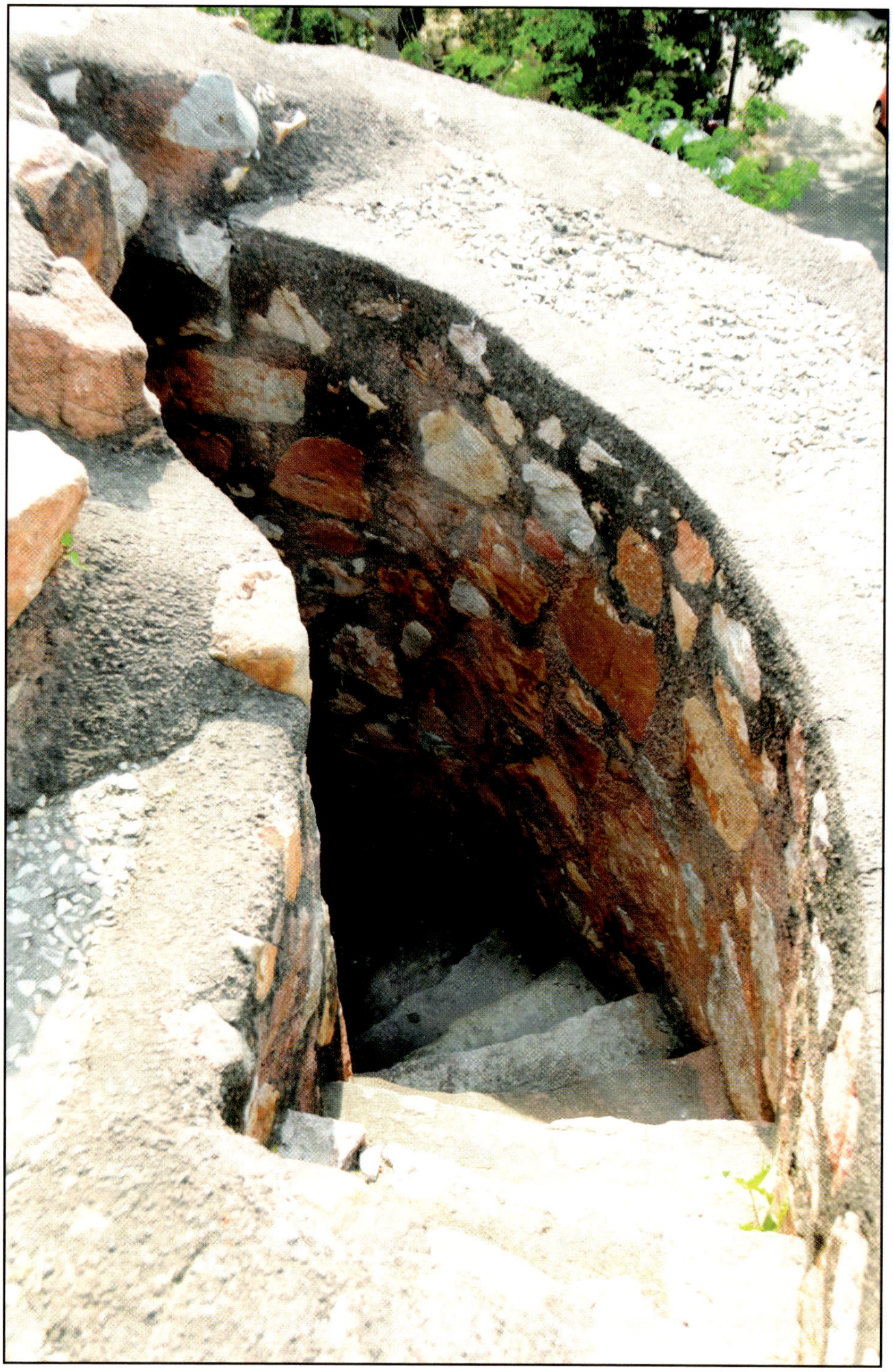

Fig. 33. Steps leading down from roof of Chor Minar.

Maulvi Zafar Hasan inspected Chor Minar in 1910 and reported "the minar, constructed of rubble masonry, stands in the centre of a platform some 30 feet square and 7 feet in height (Fig. 37). Each of the four sides of the platform has three arched recesses, the central one on the east being a doorway which

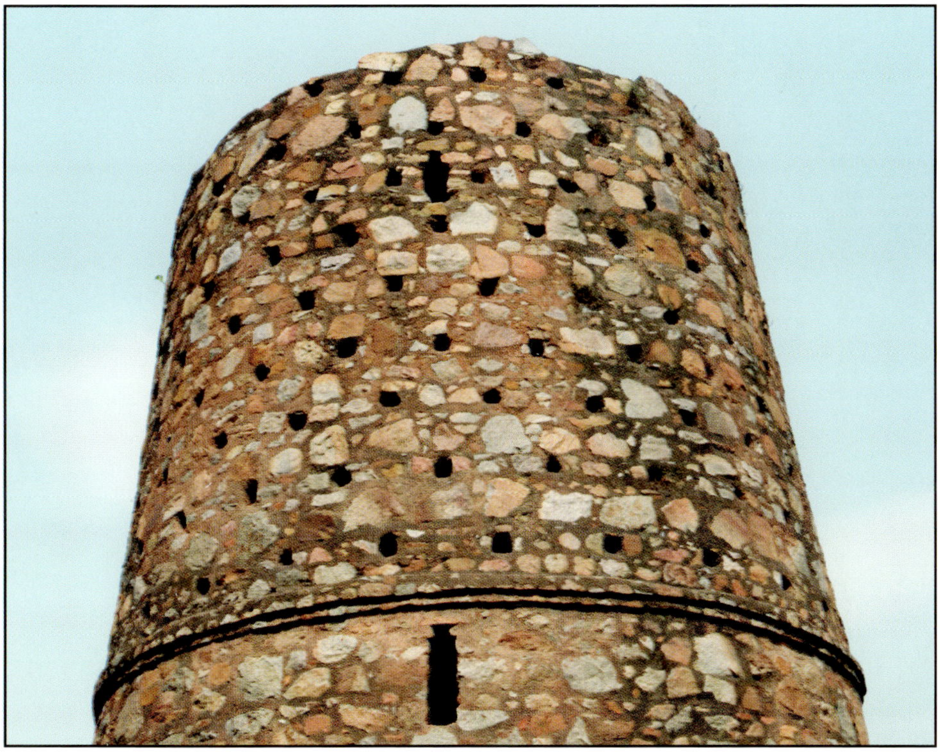

Fig. 34. Holes on the cylindrical surface of Chor Minar and oblong opening for ventilation.

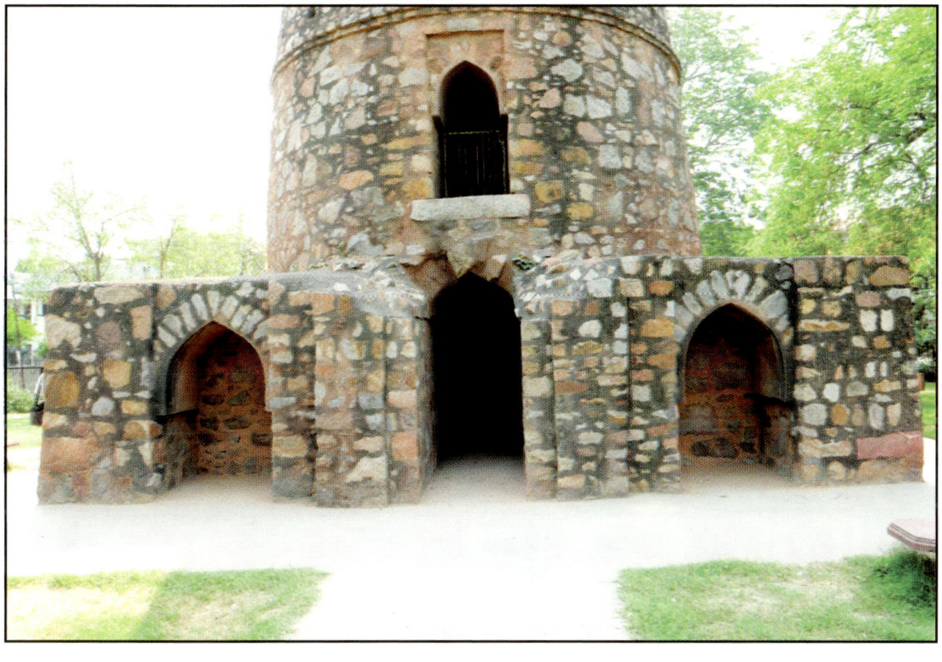

Fig. 35. Arched opening on the façade of Chor Minar.

gives access to a spiral stair leading to the top. The minar is circular in plan and tapers. The chief feature of interest is the circular holes on the external face of the structure. Traditionally it is known as Chor Minar and was built to strike terror to the thieves by whom the place was infested. Their heads are

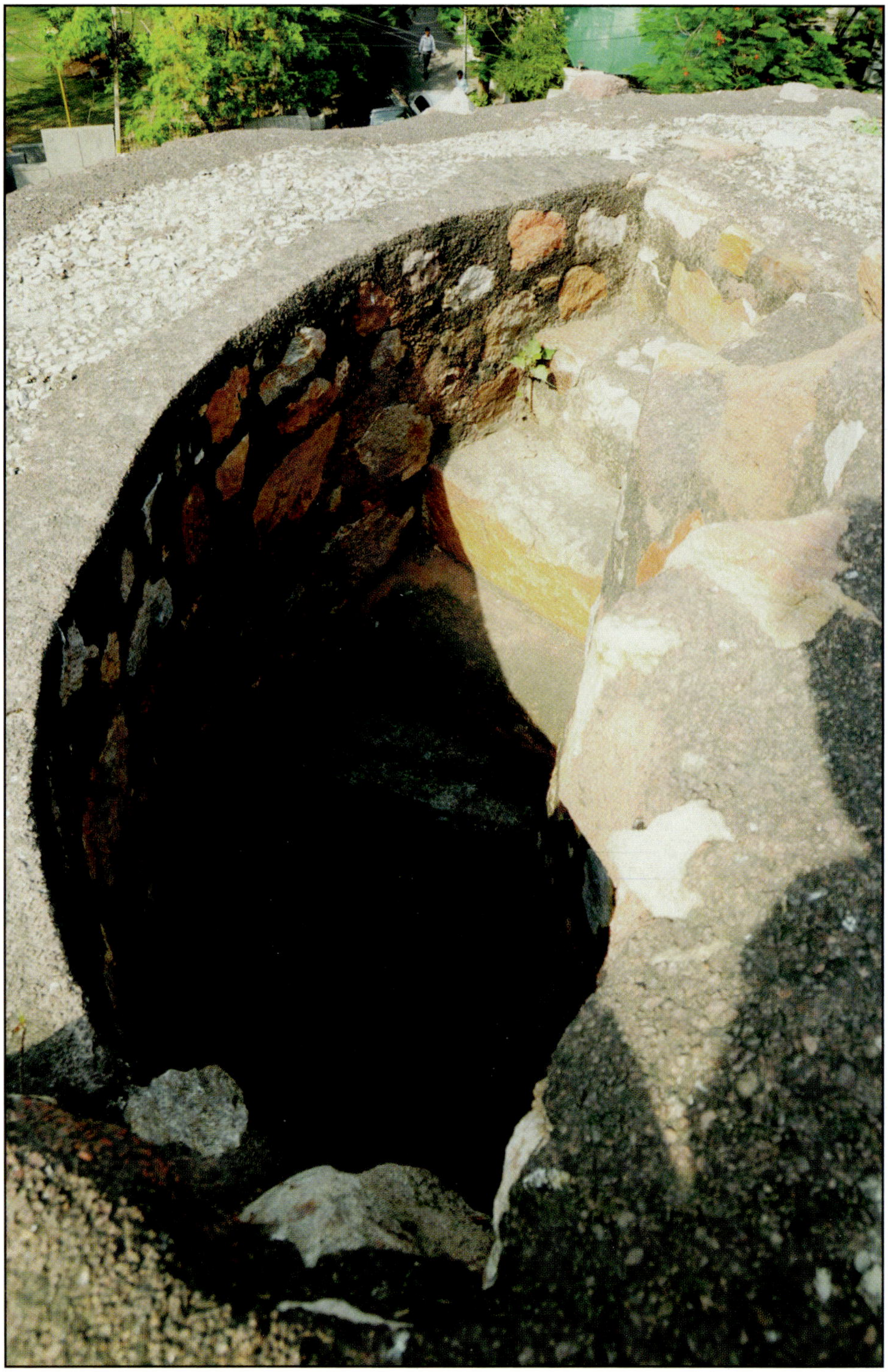

Fig. 36. Staircase indicating broken superstructure.

said to have been severed and placed for public exposure in the holes of the minar, a circumstance from which it has derived its name. Immediately to the east of the minar is a ruined wall mosque, while some 150 yards to the south lie the ruins of a baoli."[2]

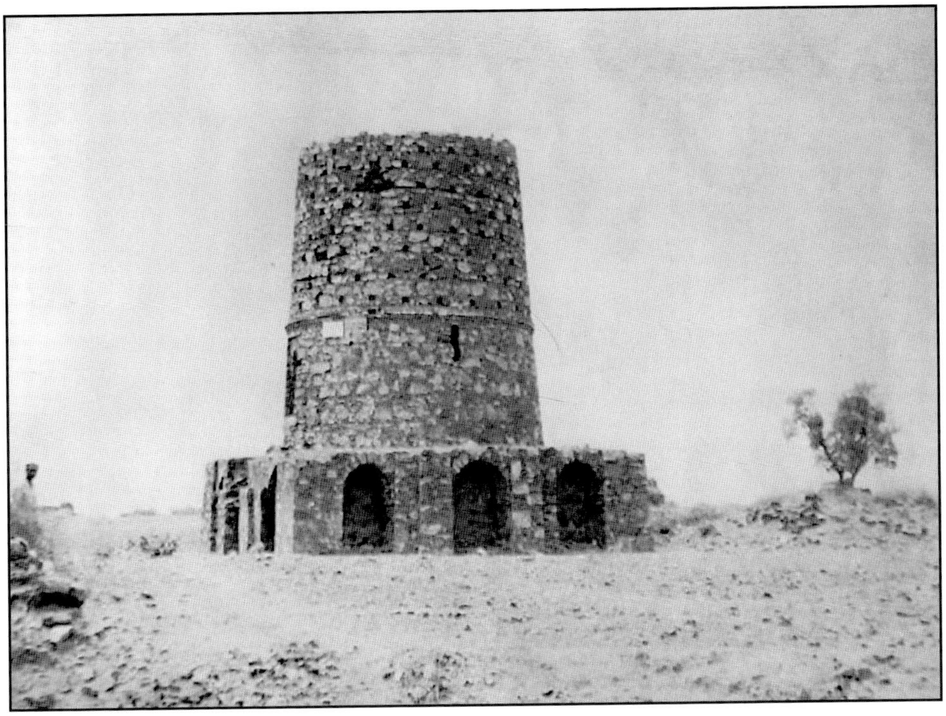

Fig. 37. Architectural form of Chor Minar.

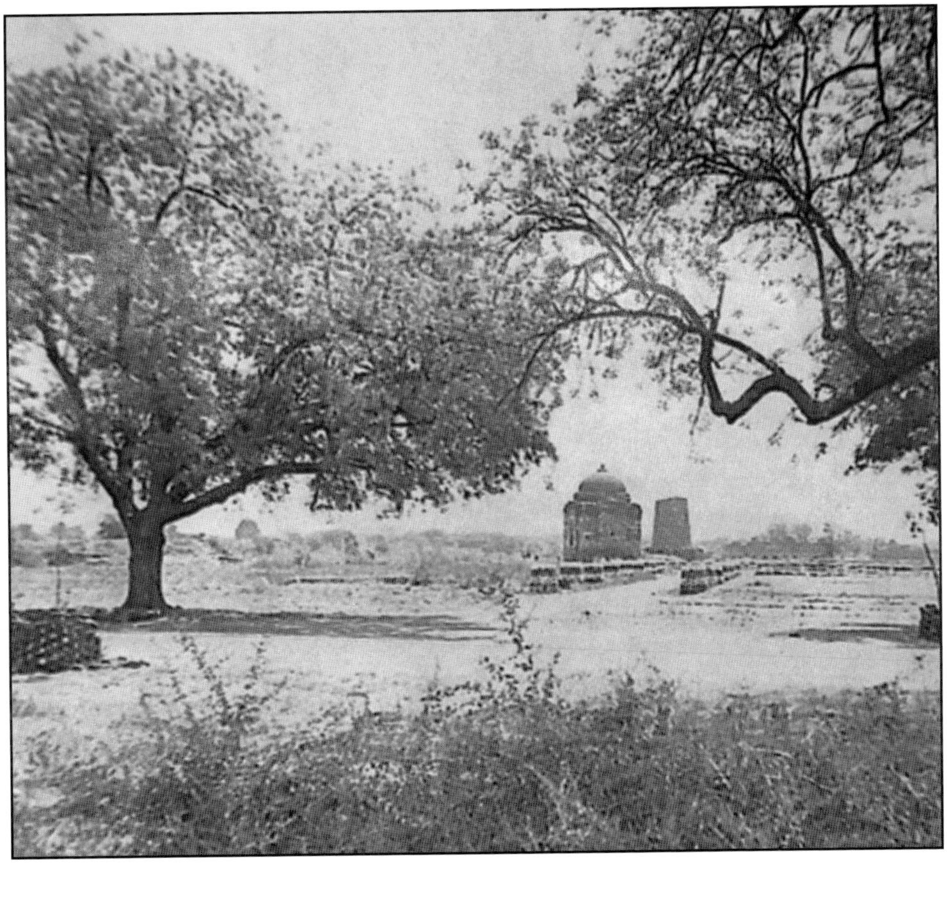

Fig. 38. The wonder that was Kharera Village.

During the course of listing the monuments in Kharera village, Maulvi Zafar Hasan mentions at serial no. 277 (a) Enclosing wall of the village, no. 278 (a) Mosque nameless, no 279 (a) Nili Masjid , no 280 (a) Tomb locally known as Bandi ka or Poti ka Gumbad, no. 281 (a) Tomb locally known as Biwi or Dadi ka Gumbad no. 282(a) Tomb locally known as Biran ka Gumbad, no.283 (a) Chhoti Gumti, no. 284 (a), Tomb locally known as Sakri Gumti, no. 285 (a) Tomb locally known as Barah Khamba, no. 286 (a) Atte wala gumbad, no 287 (a) Idgah, no. 288 (a) Tomb locally known as Idgah wala Gumbad, no. 289 (a) Chor Minar, no. 290 (a) Mosque (nameless) respectively (Fig. 38).[3] However, due to rapid and unrestricted urbanisation process, several historical monuments representing glorious past of Kharera village have been completely erased from the ground and are lost for ever.

References

1. Maulvi Zafar Hasan, *Delhi Province, List of Muhammadan and Hindu Monuments, Vol III*. Calcutta, 1922, p.166.
2. *Ibid.*
3. *Ibid.*, pp.160-167.

5 Challenges of Preservation

Kos minars are a category of architecture that developed with a clear association with road networks, since their primary function was to serve as markers and this perhaps was also their undoing. They are generally perceived as unassuming structures that were functional rather than aesthetically pleasing and hence face an uphill task in terms of survival from an ever-expanding demand for land in cities and towns. As alignments of roads changed over time, some of the kos minars were left isolated in the middle of fields, while others were demolished to make way for urban conveniences. More than any other category of monument, the conservation of kos minars perhaps poses the greatest challenge to the preservation of India's heritage.

In the nineteenth century, conservation and repair, which were looked after by local governments, had formed no part of the Archaeological Survey of India Director-General's responsibilities. This gradually changed with the passing of The Ancient Monuments Preservation Act, 1904. Under this Act, the government could acquire land for the protection of monuments under the Land Acquisition Act 1894 and issue notifications declaring the changed status of the monument. At the time of independence on August 15, 1947, a total of 2826 monuments had been declared of national importance.

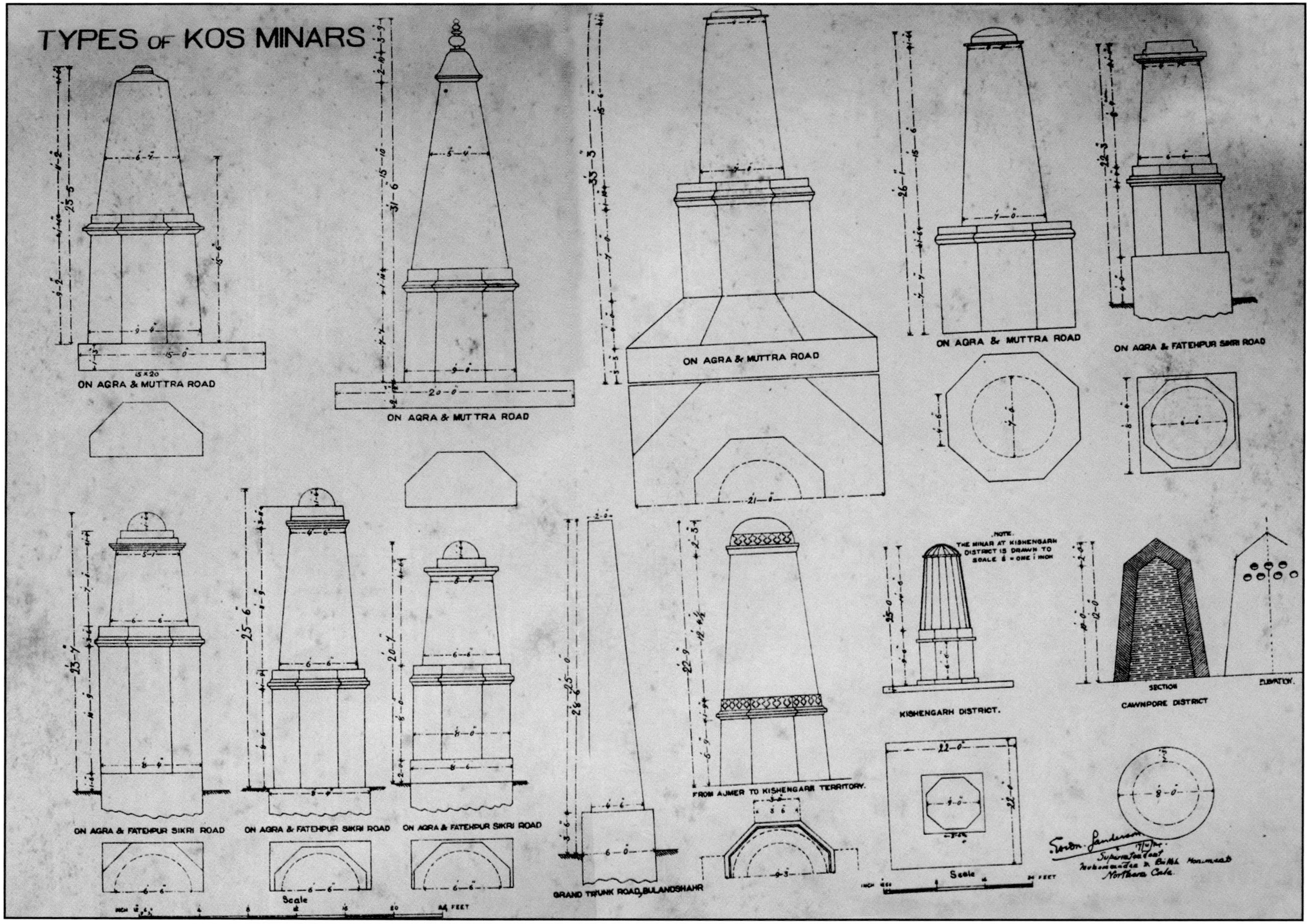

Fig. 39. Types of kos minars (Taken from: *Annual Progress Report, Superintendent, Mohammadan and British Monuments, Northern Circle, 1914, Pl. 44*).

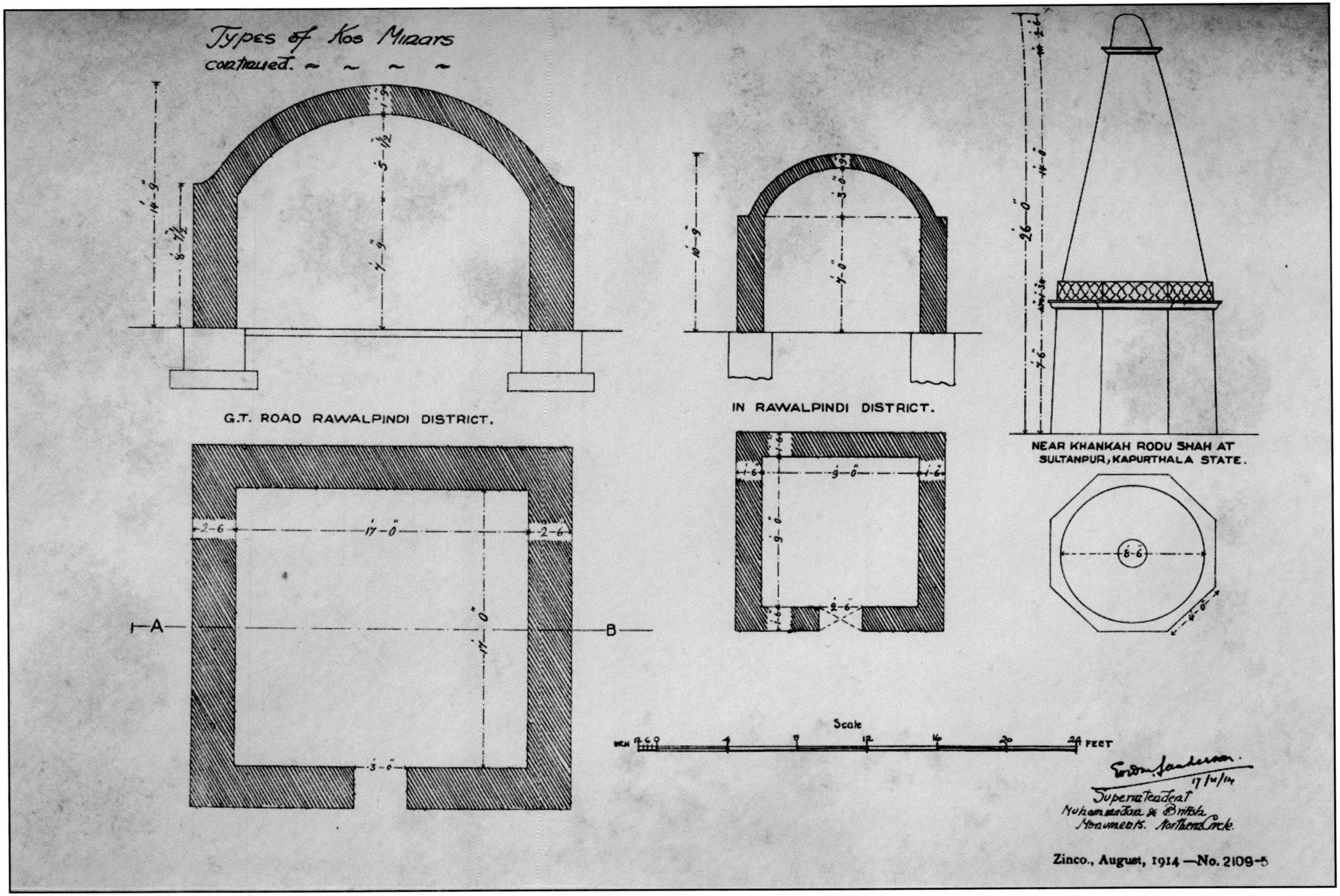

Fig. 40. Types of kos minars (continued).

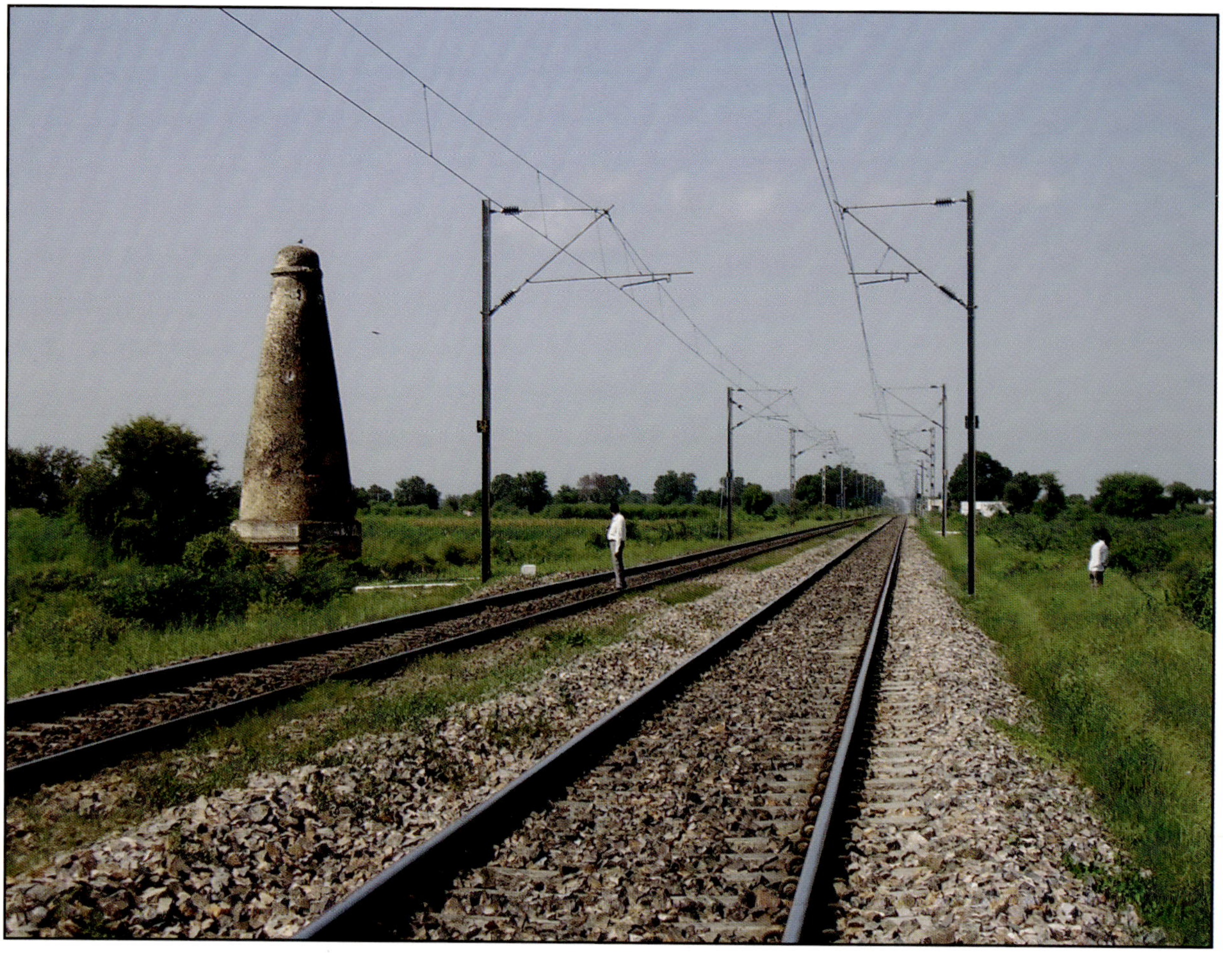

Fig. 41. The earlier highways on which the kos minars stood have now been replaced by trains, thus exposing them to constant vibrations.

Starting from 1913, when the kos minar in Delhi, now inside the precincts of the Zoological Park (Figs. 19-20) was declared protected, the number of kos minars in the list of centrally protected monuments gradually increased, though they continued to suffer under severe urban pressure. One such is located in the cloth market of Ambala city, which was notified as a protected monument in 1918 and is constantly facing the wrath of the ever expanding populace. Similarly a community centre was proposed to be built near the medieval kos minar just across the Delhi-Badarpur border, with the administration constantly struggling to clear encroachments.[1] Even in cases, such as the minar inside the zoo or another one in Bhulwana village in Palwal on the Delhi-Agra road, which are protected from encroachments and vandalism, they have lost their context and stand isolated with little purpose or direction. In other cases roads and railway lines run in close proximity to the minars with the vibrations and the pollutants from vehicular traffic being constant threats.

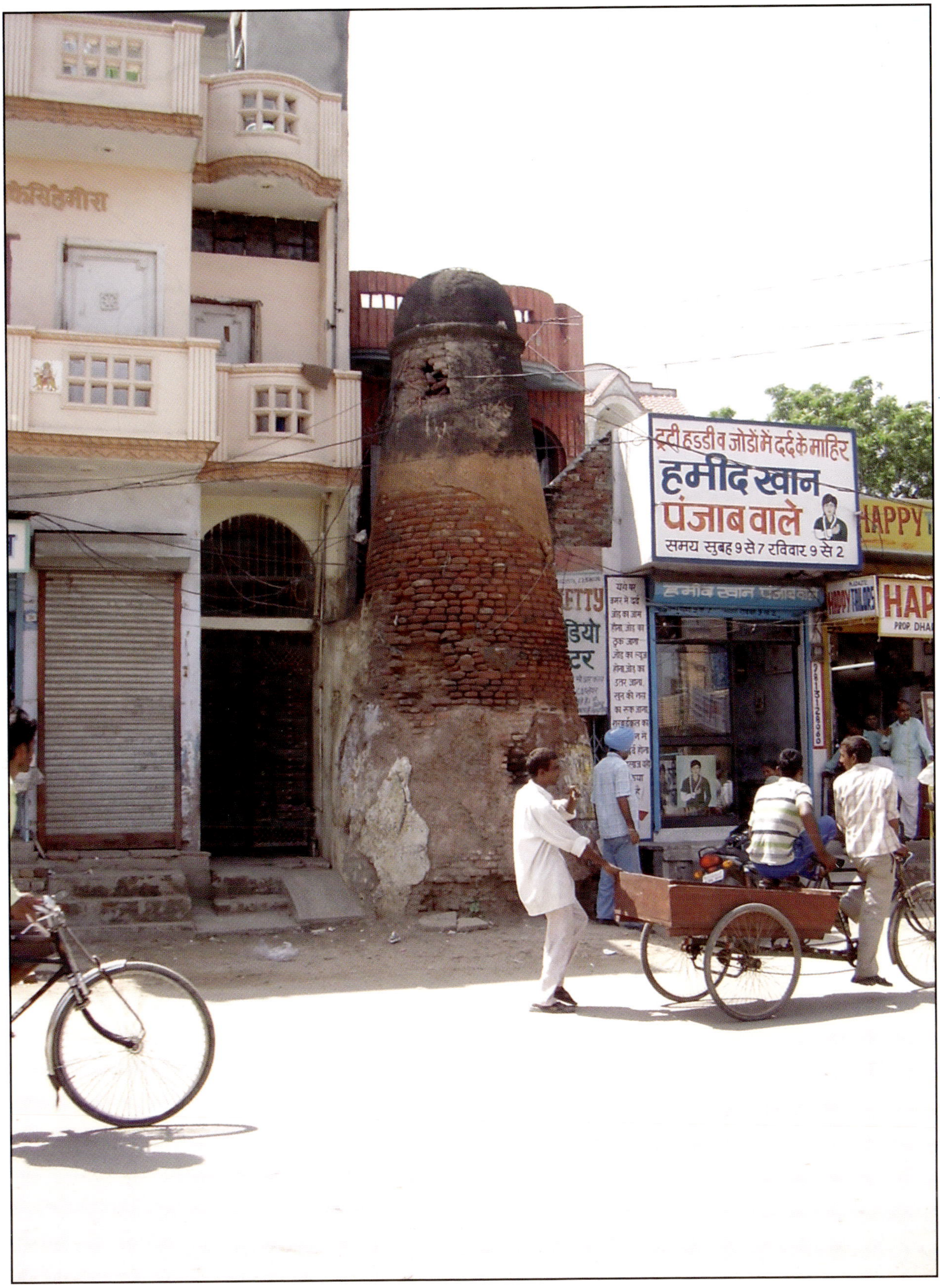

Fig. 42. Kos Minar at Sonepat hemmed in by structures.

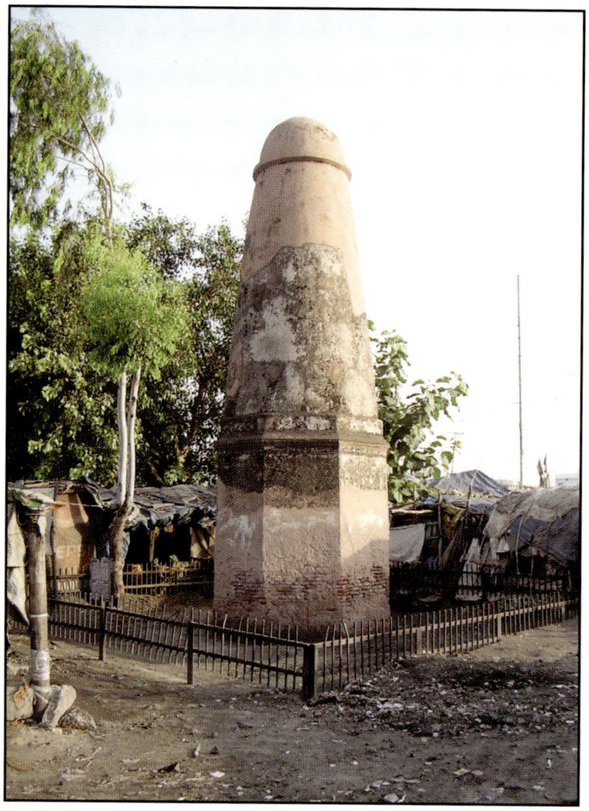

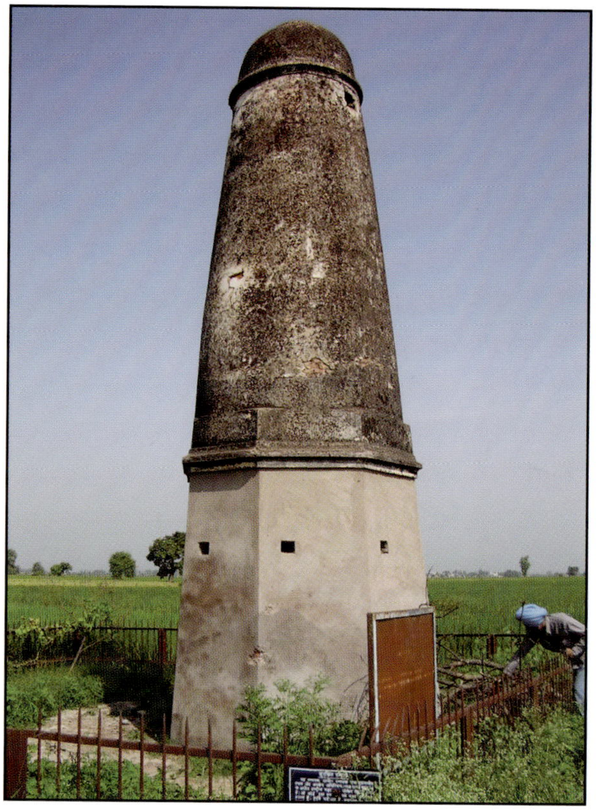

Left: **Fig. 43.** Settlement around the kos minar. Fortunately the protected area around it has been demarcated by a railing.

Right: **Fig. 44.** Kos Minar standing in the fields within its defined space. The ASI's board clearly indicates its protected status.

Fortunately the courts have often come to the support of the kos minars. The Delhi High Court ordered the authorities to clear encroachments around the Mathura Road kos minar at Badarpur.[2] In another case, the Rajasthan High Court issued instructions to authorities on a Public Interest Litigation with regard to the kos minar situated at Moti Doongri Road at Shiv colony near Sanganer Gate, which was in shambles.[3]

In section 49 of the Indian Constitution, our founding fathers accepted that "it shall be the obligation of the State to protect every monument or place or object of artistic or historical interest, declared by or under law made by Parliament to be of national importance, from spoliation, disfigurement, destruction, removal, disposal or export, as the case may be". This is however a daunting objective that the Government of India has consistently striven to achieve, as evident from the enactment of the Ancient Monuments and Archaeological Sites and Remains AMASR (Amendment and Validation) Act, 2010 which was enacted in March, 2010. The 2010 Act provides statutory provision for 100 meter prohibited and 100 to 300 meters regulated areas around the monument, with a complete ban on construction in the prohibited area. It is hoped that these measures will ameliorate the conditions around kos minars.

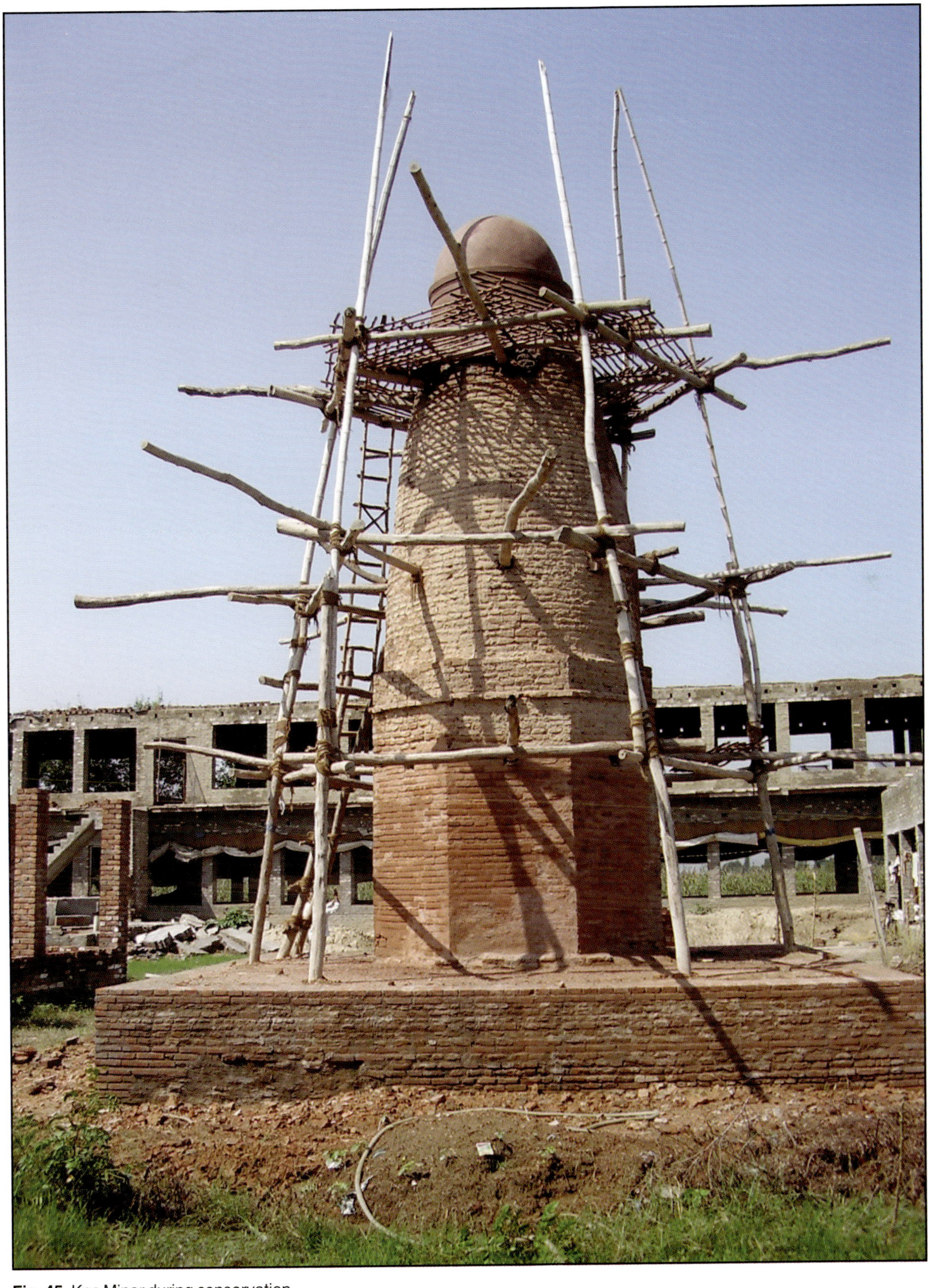

Fig. 45. Kos Minar during conservation.

References

1. R.V. Smith, On the Meandering Highway of History, *The Hindu*, Delhi, Monday June 27, 2005.
2. C.D. Verma, Signposts Lost in History, *The Tribune*, Sunday September 10, 2006.
3. HC Notice on Kos Minar Condition, *The Times of India*, Jaipur, July 3, 2012.

6 Conclusion

All above minars have gateways and spiral staircase leading to top. The cupola (*chhatri*) of Hiran Minar is still intact, whereas the *chhatri* of Chor Minar, appears to have fallen. Externally Chor Minar is pierced

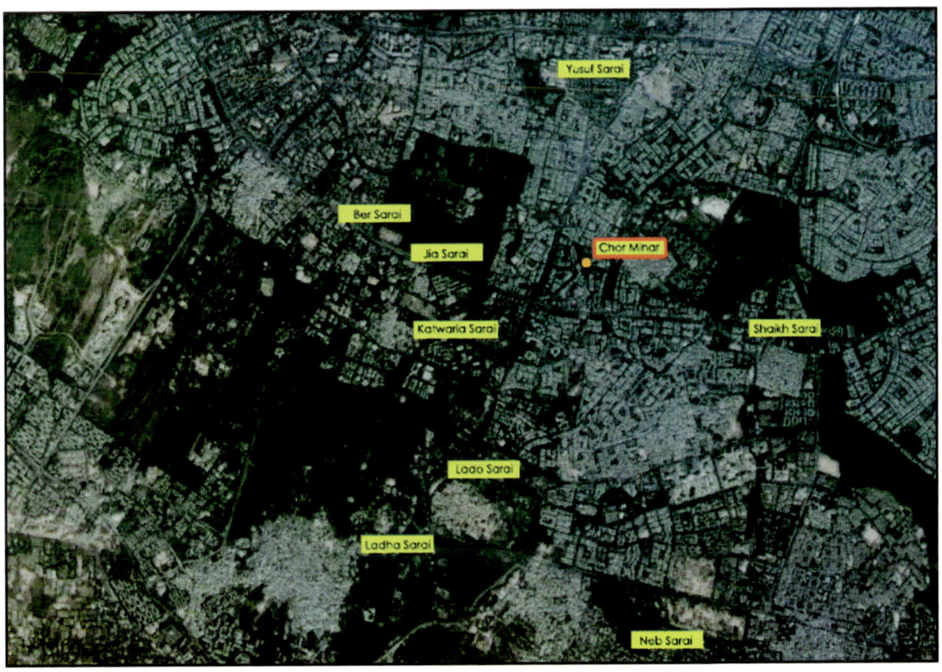

Fig. 46. Sarais in vicinity of Chor Minar are testimony to the thriving culture.

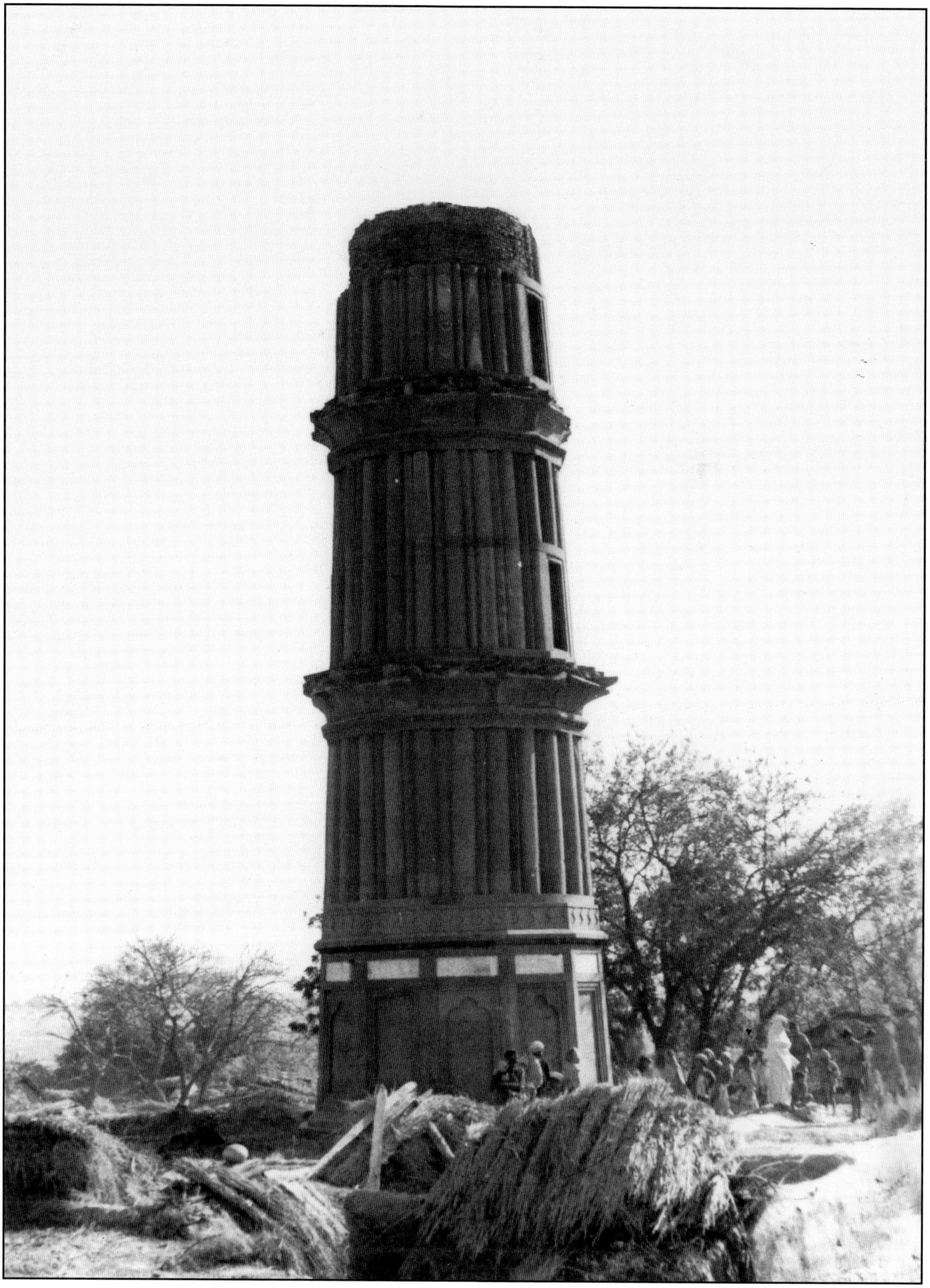

Fig. 47. Hashtsal Minar: Then (c. 1950).

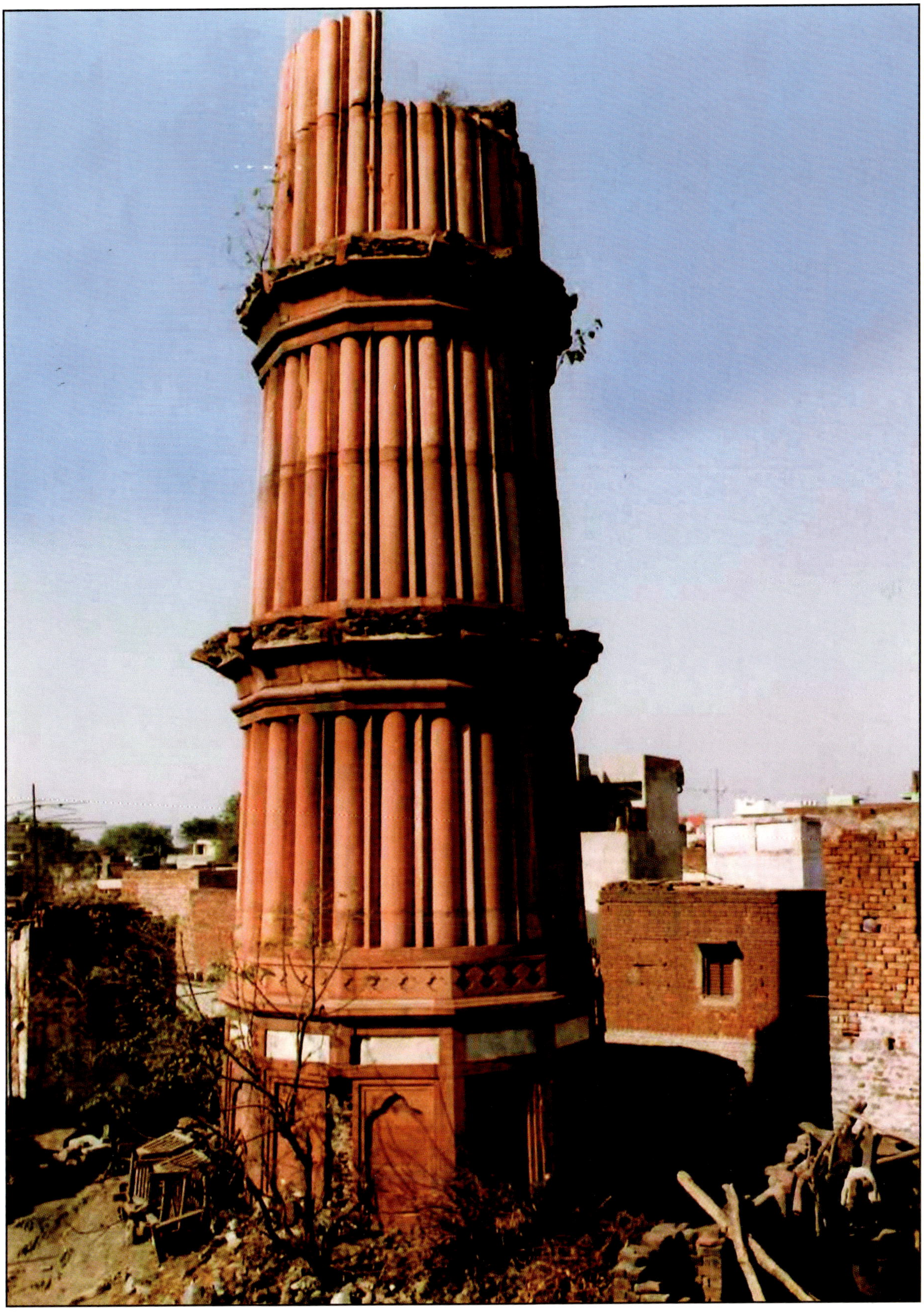

Fig. 48. Hashtsal Minar: Now.

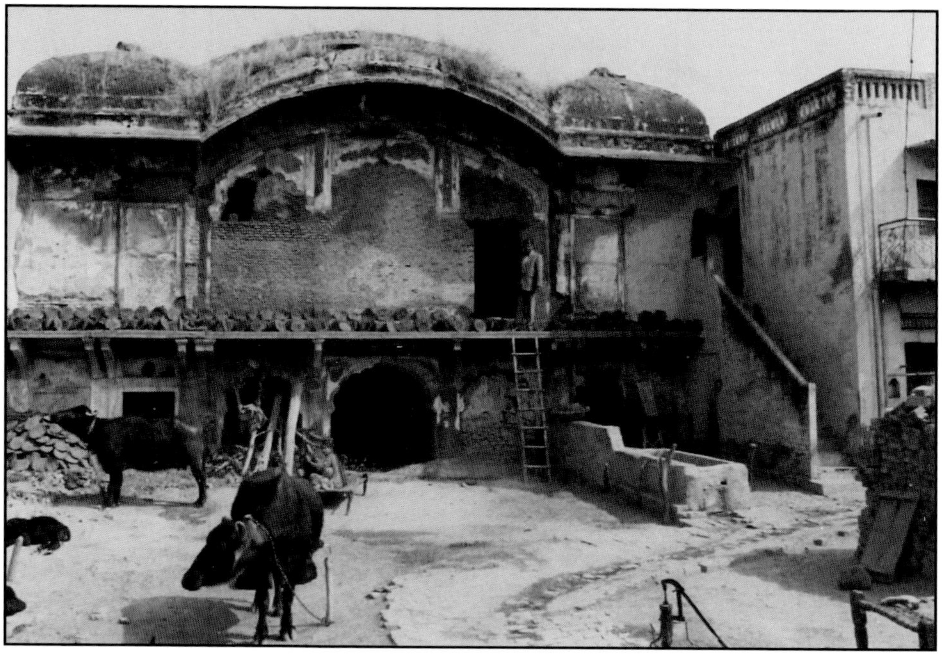

Fig. 49. Shikarkhas Kanonda, Jaunti village.

with several holes probably to set in stone replicas of antelope horns or elephant's teeth or may be different bits and pieces. Such type of architectural decoration is unique and found in kos minars purposefully. Perhaps, such decorations were helpful in identifying a particular minar as an important landmark either at the beginning of the journey point or at the end, or otherwise of immense historical importance. The architecture of Chor Minar and its ambiance was studied carefully which reveals close resemblance with Hiran

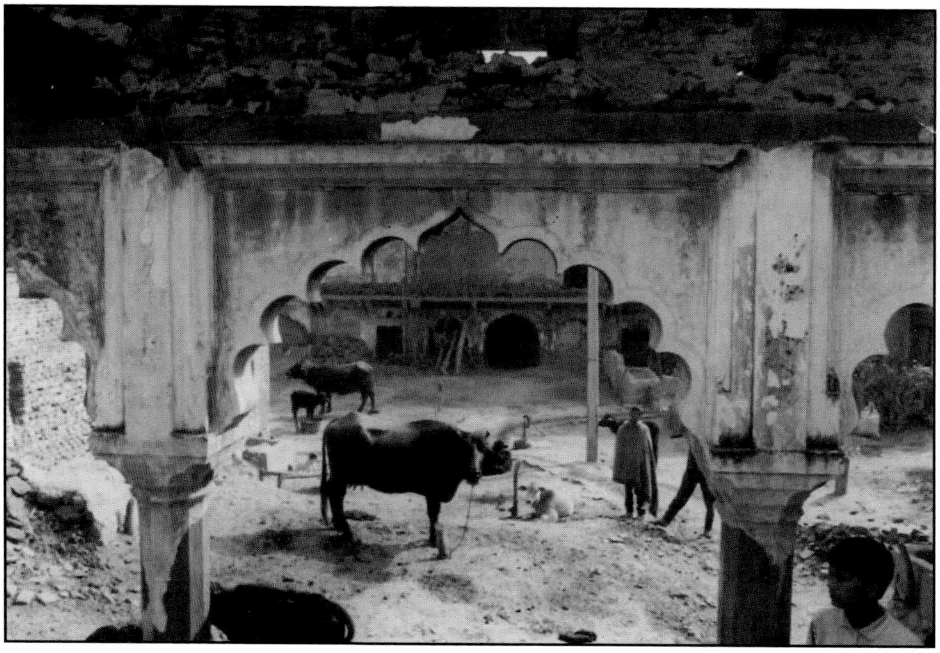

Fig. 50. Architectural remains of Shikarkhas (hunting lodge) complex.

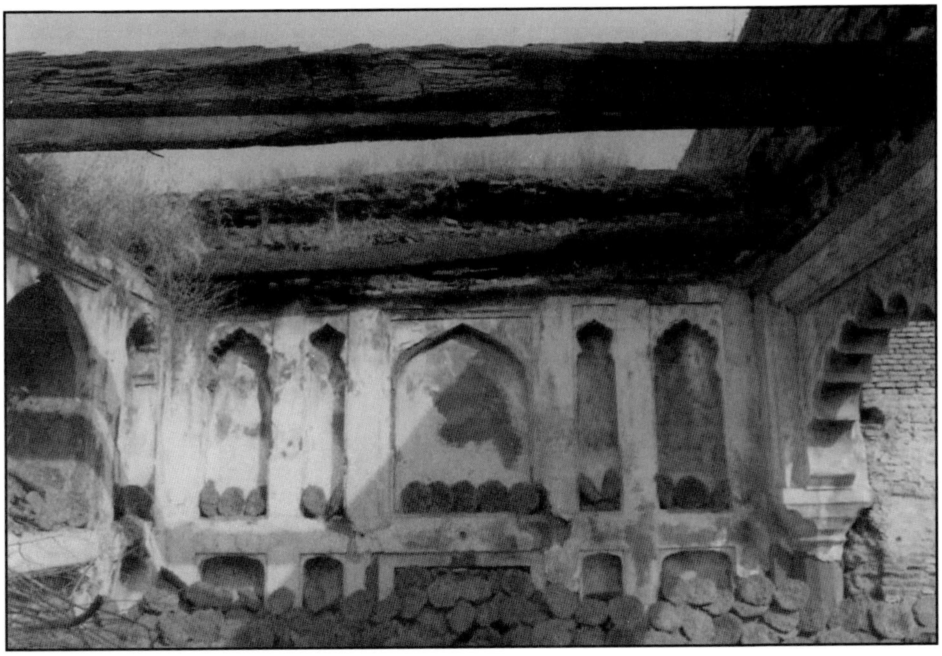

Fig. 51. Remains of interior: Jaunti Shikarkhas.

Minar of Fatehpur Sikri. The most remarkable feature of Fatehpur Sikri's Hiran Minar was provision of inbuilt drinking water management system and outlet of water through underground channel for storing it in adjoining tank. Hiran Minar served dual purpose. It was a significant kos minar as well as a *pyau*.

Its location was in front of principal entrance to the city which became memorable landmark to the travellers. In fact, it was the first kos minar on route leading to Ajmer or Delhi from Fatehpur Sikri and equipped with adequate

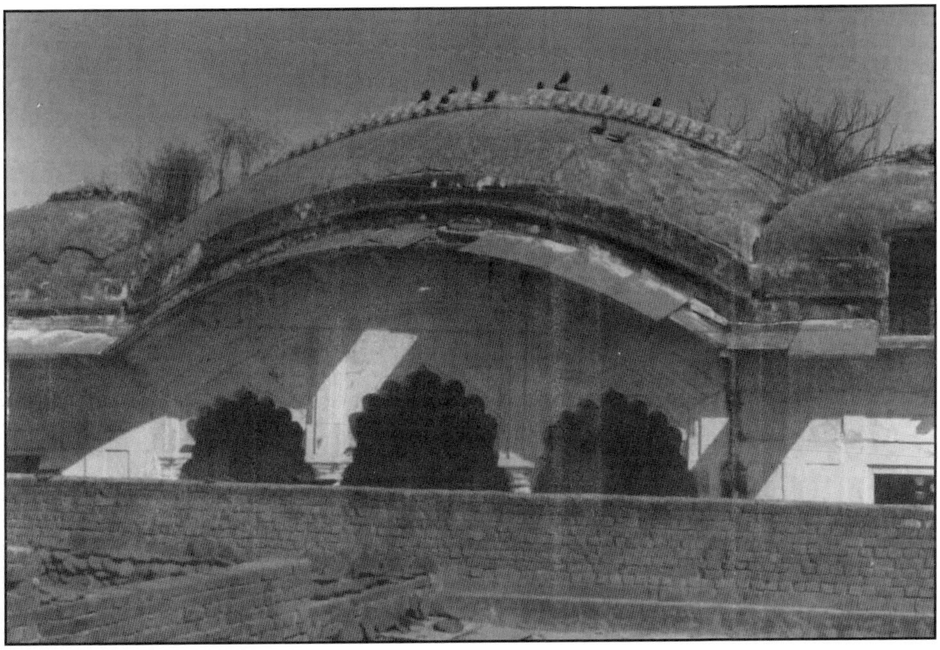

Fig. 52. Palam Shikargah.

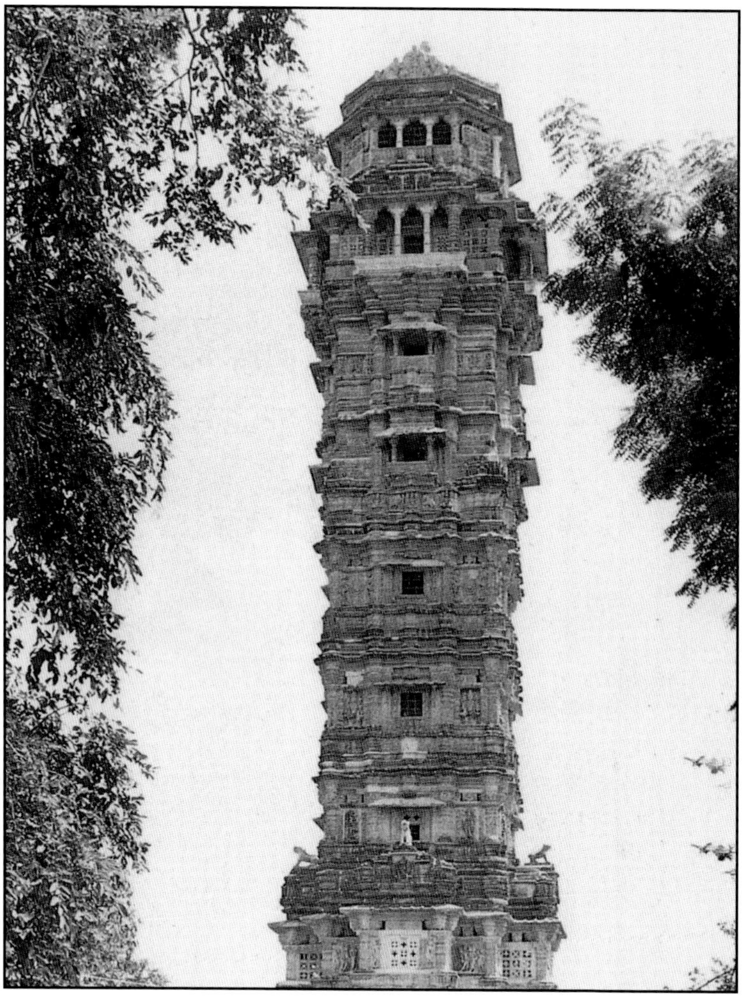

Fig. 53. Kirttistambha, Chittorgarh Fort.

facilities. Likewise, Chor Minar was an important kos minar and prime landmark for travellers who began journey or ended it near Siri. It is significant that there were several *caravansarais* located in its vicinity and still known with their original names i.e. *Yusuf Sarai, Jia Sarai, Katwaria Sarai, Ber Sarai, Laddha Sarai, Lado Sarai* so on and so forth (Fig. 46).

Undoubtedly, these well known *sarais* (inns) were utilised as boarding / lodging places for night stay by the travellers. Therefore, the availability of several *caravansarais* in the vicinity of Chor Minar further substantiate our standpoint regarding their situation on ancient trade route at considerable distance. Within the vicinity of Chor Minar, three more monuments namely *Idgah, Baoli* and Mosque are situated in the revenue boundary of ancient Kharera village. It seems, these monuments were also an integral part of contemporary trade and trade route system.

The comprehensive field survey, historical study and architectural enumeration of Hiran Minar, Neem Sarai Minar and Chor Minar have revealed without any ambiguity that these minars were originally constructed as exceptional kos minars and subsequently derived their nomenclature in due course of time.

Apart from these, few more important minars (towers) of medieval period are mentionworthy in this context. Amongst them, one is Hashtsal Minar situated in Hashtsal village near Palam (Figs. 47-48). It was constructed during the reign of Shahjahan and architecturally resembles Qutb Minar.[1] Although, architecture and style of construction of Hashtsal Minar closely resembles Qutb Minar, but functionally its purpose was altogether different. In fact, it was a shooting tower near *Shikargah* (hunting lodge) at Palam, constructed near Shahjahanabad in addition to *Shikarkhas* of village Kanonda (presently in Jaunti village), at a distance of fifteen *kos (kuroh)* from *Dar-ul-Hukumat* (Shahjahanabad).

Abdul Hamid Lahori (contemporary court historian of Shahjahan) categorically mentioned about several visits of emperor Shahjahan and heir apparent Dara Shikoh to these *shikarkhas* for royal hunting expeditions (Figs. 49-52). The literary references and architectural style of this minar speaks a lot about its use and purpose.

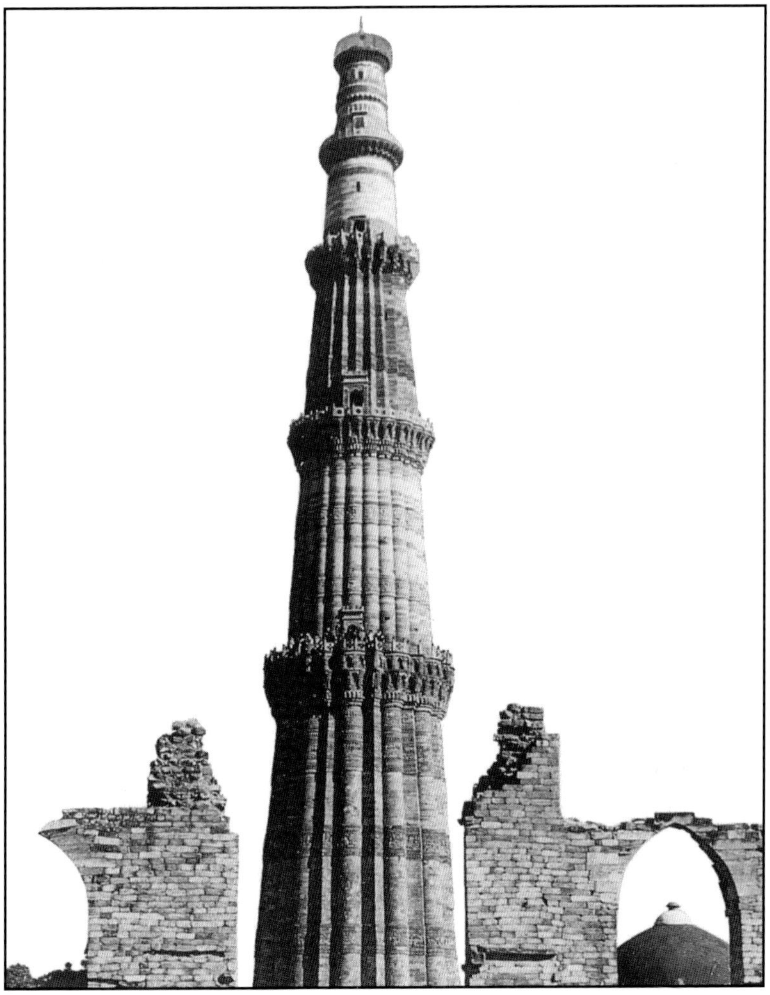

Fig. 54. Qutb Minar, Mehrauli.

Several other minars / towers during medieval period were constructed but with altogether different ideas, symbolism, aims and objectives. For example, *Kirttistambha* (Fig. 53) of Maharana Kumbha at Chittorgarh Fort, Qutb Minar (Fig. 54) at Mehrauli arc noteworthy. Both these monuments (towers) were built in accordance with tradition and essential requirement of the state to commemorate ideas, theory and wisdom symbolising *'Doctrine of Kinship'*. It is unfortunate that the wonderful *Kirttistambha* of Chittorgarh is popularly understood to be a Victory Tower and it is generally called by the misnomer *Vijayastambha*. The *Kirttistambha* is not a military relic, symbolising a mundane thing. The deep-rooted concept, meaning and purpose which led Kumbha and his architects to conceive, plan and build it in such an intelligent and magnificent way has been lost in the debris. The textual references show that the mythological *'Mahameru'* which has been referred to in the various epigraphs of the *Kirttistambha* and which is indeed a prefix of the *Kirttistambha* i.e. *Mahameru-Kirttistambha* as the highest representation of the phenomenal world, that is *jagat* viz. *trailokya* consisting of 21 *lokas* in the three worlds (*patala, mrityu* or *bhu* and *svarga*) and it is the abode of Gods and Goddesses.

The *Kirttistambha* is the architectural representation of the *Puranic Mahameru*. But it is not *Mahameru* alone, it is also a *Kirttistambha*.[2] Since present research does not cover architectural and historical enumeration of above monuments, they are left out from the purview of the present study.

Besides kos minars and other associated edifices constructed along the ancient trade route and communication system, one more historical monument needs special attention and is mentionworthy in this context. It is popularly known as Maqbara Paik (Fig. 55) located on G.T. Karnal Bye Pass road crossing, Delhi. This octagonal tomb (*Maqbara Payak*) is a solitary and noteworthy example of monuments built on ancient trade route. Architecturally, it belongs to Pathan period and known as "Maqbara Paik" since Maulvi Zafar Hasan recorded (1908) it accordingly. The word "paik" seems to be a corrupt form of Persian word *payak* (messenger) which has been wrongly spelled by J.A. Page and J.F. Blakiston during the compilation of publication, *List of Muhammadan and Hindu Monuments*. In fact, it appears to be a tomb of an unidentified important person/officer who died while performing his duty at this spot as a royal messenger. It is quite probable that this magnificent monument was erected in his honour, perhaps by a royal order. This is how it became an integral part of the monuments associated with ancient routes and communication system of medieval India.

Modestly, above observation is purely based upon field survey and comprehensive study of kos minar's architecture as reflected in its style and construction. Be that as it may, there is no last word in history, even if claimed to be so. Therefore, future research on the subject will certainly advance above study further from the stage where art historians have left it. There are several monuments in India wrongly popularised and are still famous with different names such as *Kala Gumbad, Choti Gumti, Sabj Burz, Sakri Gumti, Adhai Din Ka Jhopra, Hiran Minar, Neem Sarai, Chor Minar* etc. It is essential to set the historical record straight related to these monuments with their original name and proper identification, on the basis of architecture, history, archaeology and literary references combined. The present study is an attempt in this direction. The response of the scholarly world is anticipated on the subject with healthy criticism.

It is also pertinent to mention here that the Heritage Bye-Laws related to each monument are under preparation. The present research carried out by NMA in this regard would be of immense importance to visualise historical identity and personality of each monument in proper perspective. Therefore,

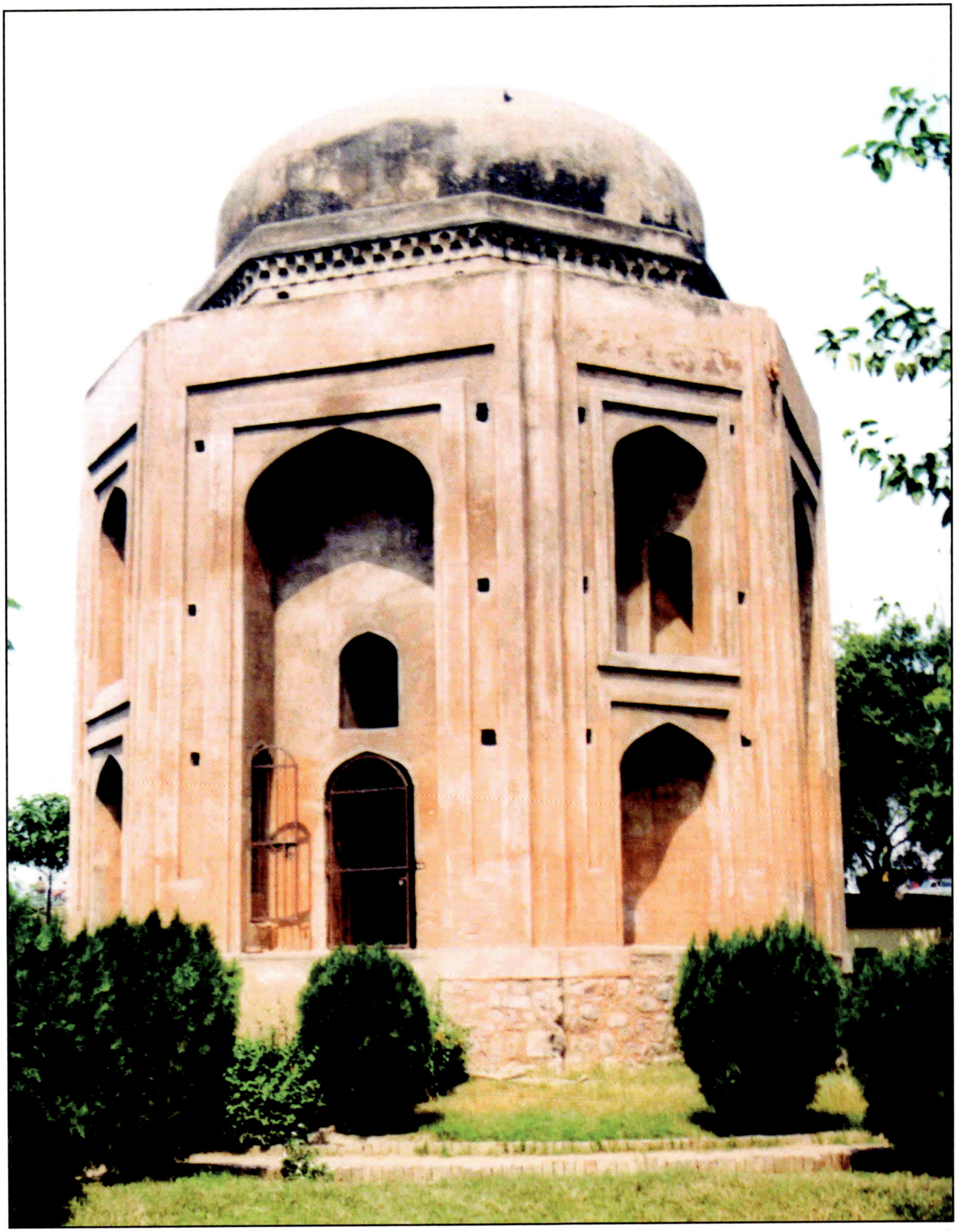

Fig. 55. Maqbara Payak, Delhi.

the above analytical study will provide guidelines to the officers who have been assigned responsibility of framing the Heritage Bye-Laws.

References

1. Y. D. Sharma, *Delhi and Its Neighbourhood.* New Delhi, 2001, p.132.
2. R. Nath, *Chittorgarh Kirttistambha of Maharana Kumbha*, New Delhi,1999, p.68.

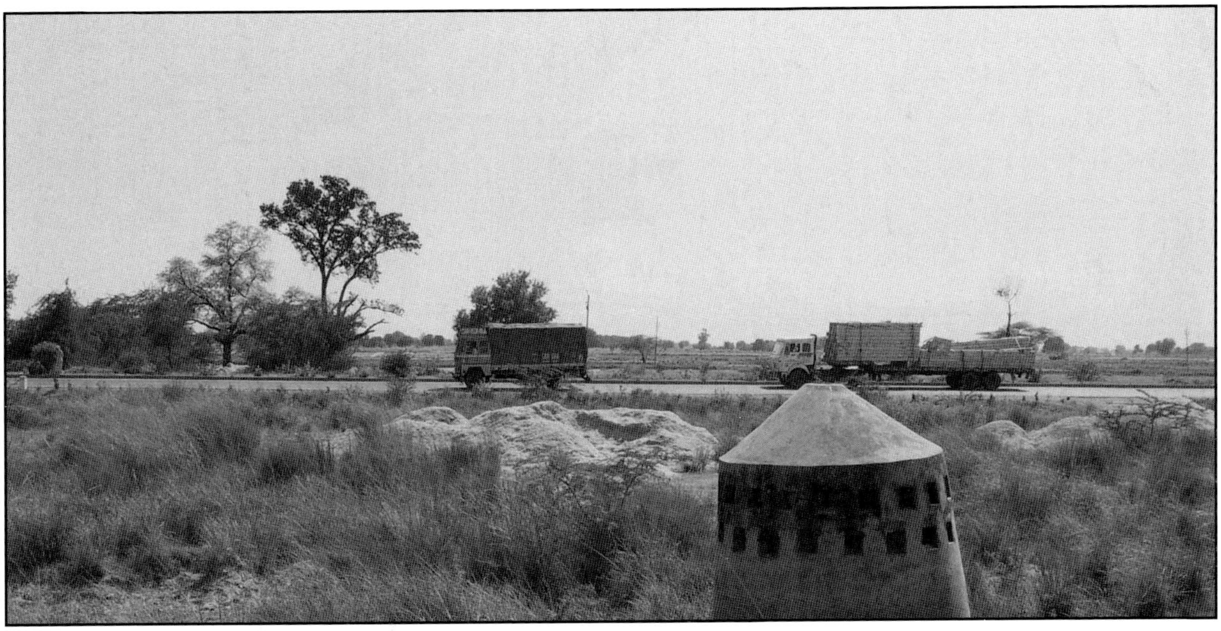

Appendix I

Year Wise Notifications of 110 Kos Minars Protected by Archaeological Survey of India

DELHI

Kos Minar Notified in Year 1913

1. **Babarpur/Kakanagar (Zoo)** kos minar (Lat.28°36'N; Long. 77°14'E) was notified vide notification no. DI.1717-Edu. dated 01.03.1913. Located within the premises of Delhi Zoo.

HARYANA

Kos Minars Notified in Year 1914

1. **Bheni-Kalan**, Karnal kos minar (Lat 29°45'N; Long 76°56'E) was notified vide notification no. PN 1083 dated 1.12.1914. Located 3 km west of NH-1 on Bheni Kalan-Sultanpur Road. Its upper portion is partly broken.
2. **Daha**, Karnal kos minar (Lat 29°38'N; Long 76°59'E) was notified vide notification no. PN 1083 dated 1.12.1914. Located in the middle of present road.
3. **Gharaunda (North)** kos minar (Lat 29°33'N; Long 76°59'E) was notified vide notification no. PN 1083 dated 1.12.1914. Located between town and railway line.

4. **Gharaunda (South)** kos minar (Lat 29°33'N; Long 76°59'E) was notified vide notification no. PN 1083 dated 1.12.1914. Located to the south of the town.
5. **Karnal (Namaste Chowk),** kos minar (Lat 29°40'N; Long 77°00'E) was notified vide notification no. PN 1083 dated 1.12.1914. Located near Namaste Chowk in Sector 4, Transport Nagar.
6. **Karnal (Karnal City),** kos minar (Lat 29°42'N; Long 76°58'E) was notified vide notification no. PN 1083 dated 1.12.1914. Located in the centre of city, near the Gate no. 2 of National Dairy Research Institute. Its plaster at severalparts has peeled off.
7. **Kohand**, Karnal kos minar (Lat 29°29'N; Long 76°58'E) was notified vide notification no. PN 1083 dated 1.12.1914. It is of standard design and located to south of the town.
8. **Tirawari (Taraori, North)**, Karnal kos minar (Lat 29°49'N; Long 76°55'E) was notified vide notification no. PN 1083 dated 1.12.1914. Located about 3km north of Taraori village, on Taraori-Ajanthali Road.
9. **Tirawari(Taraori, South),** Karnal kos minar (Lat 29°49'N; Long 76°55'E) was notified vide notification no. PN 1083 dated 1.12.1914. It stands near NH -1and is located on Nadana Road.
10. **Amin,** Kurukshetra kos minar (Lat 29°53'N; Long 76°52'E) was notified vide notification no. PN 1083 dated 1.12.1914. According to Subhash Parihar it is located between Amin and Barthal, on the side of road (Parihar, 2008:184). Its cylindrical part is not so high in comparison to other kos minars, which overall gives it stout appearance.
11. **Adhor/Adhaun**, Kurukshetra kos minar (Lat 30° 02'N; Long 76°50'E) was notified vide notification no. PN 1083 dated 1.12.1914. Located in the fields on the road to Dhauni.
12. **Bhiwani Khera**, Kurukshetra kos minar (Lat 30°00'N; Long 76°52'E) was notified vide notification no. PN 1083 dated 1.12.1914. Located on periphery of the village, in the field.
13. **Fatuhpur**, Kurukshetra kos minar (Lat 29°51'N; Long 76°55'E) was notified vide notification no. PN 1083 dated 1.12.1914. It is located in fields and in fair condition, required repairing.
14. **Mohri**, Kurukshetra kos minar (Lat 30°15'N; Long 76°51'E) was notified vide notification no. PN 1083 dated 1.12.1914. Located before the village, between NH-1 and railway line. In fair condition, plaster peeled off in some parts.
15. **Thanesar**, Kurukshetra kos minar (Lat 29°58'N; Long 76°50'E) was notified vide notification no. PN 1083 dated 1.12.1914. Located on Salarpur Road, adjoining Singla Rice Mill. Not in good condition, base crumbling.

16. **Sarai Sukhi**, Kurukshetra kos minar (Lat 30°04'N; Long 76°50'E) was notified vide notification no. PN 1083 dated 1.12.1914. Subhash Parihar mentioned it as Dhirpur kos minar, located near Railway Station (Parihar, 2008:188). Its plaster peeled off from several parts.
17. **Shahabad**, Kurukshetra kos minar (Lat 30°10'N; Long 76°52'E) was notified vide notification no. PN 1083 dated 1.12.1914. Not traceable.
18. **Zainpura**, Kurukshetra kos minar (Lat 30°12'N; Long 76°51'E) was notified vide notification no. PN 1083 dated 1.12.1914. Located in NE of the village and east of NH-1.
19. **Jatipur**, Panipat kos minar (Lat 29°18'N; Long 77°00'E) was notified vide notification no. PN 1083 dated 1.12.1914. Located near milestone Delhi 55 miles (88-89km).
20. **Kiwana**, Panipat kos minar (Lat 29°12'N; Long 77°00'E) was notified vide notification no. PN 1083 dated 1.12.1914. Located near the village Jurasi.
21. **Manana**, Panipat kos minar (Lat 29°16'N; Long 77°00'E) was notified vide notification no. PN 1083 dated 1.12.1914. Located near the village Manana.
22. **Panipat** kos minar (Lat 29°24'N; Long 76°59'E) was notified vide notification no. PN 1083 dated 1.12.1914. In some reports this kos minar is referred to as Taraf Afghana. It is located in Ramnagar, Shivalewali Gali, inside a temple precinct.
23. **Panipat** kos minar (Lat 29°24'N; Long 76°59'E) was notified vide notification no. PN 1083 dated 1.12.1914.
24. **Taraf Unsar**, Panipat kos minar (Lat 29°24'N; Long 76°59'E) was notified vide notification no. PN 1083 dated 1.12.1914. Located in Sector 25, part II. A noteworthy feature of this kos minar is a row of sunken panel near the top of the octagonal base. Although it is in good condition but some bricks from base are missing.
25. **Siwah/Siwali**, Panipat kos minar (Lat 29°20'N; Long 77°00'E) was notified vide notification no. PN 1083 dated 1.12.1914. Located near Dullapur.

Kos Minars Notified in Year 1918

26. **Ambala City** kos minar (Lat.30°23'N; Long. 76°46'E) was notified vide notification no. PN.14519 dated 29.07.1918.
27. **Akbarpur Barota**, Sonepat kos minar (Lat. 28°54'N; Long. 77°04'E) was notified vide notification no. PN.10699 dated 08.05.1918. Located in between railway line and NH-1; between Narela and Sonepat.
28. **Baiyanpur**, Sonepat kos minar (Lat. 28°58'N; Long. 77°02'E) was notified vide notification no. PN.10699 dated 08.05.1918. Located in between railway line and NH-1 in between Narela and Sonepat.

29. **Gannaur**, Sonepat kos minar (Lat.29°09'N; Long. 77°01'E) was notified vide notification no. PN.10699 dated 08.05.1918. Located north of Gannaur Railway Station.
30. **Jagdishpur**, Sonepat kos minar (Lat.28°56'N; Long. 77°04'E) was notified vide notification no. PN.10699 dated 08.05.1918. Located north of Gannaur Railway Station.
31. **Jawahari**, Sonepat kos minar (Lat.29°02'N; Long. 77°01'E) was notified vide notification no. PN.10699 dated 08.05.1918. Located 3.5 km north of Sonepat; in between railway line and NH-1.
32. **Panchi Gujran**, Sonepat kos minar (Lat.29°07'N; Long. 77°01'E) was notified vide notification no. PN.10699 dated 08.05.1918.
33. **Rajpur**, Sonepat kos minar (Lat.29°05'N; Long. 77°01'E) was notified vide notification no. PN.10699 dated 08.05.1918. Located 3.5 km North of Jawahari and West of railway line.
34. **Sonepat** kos minar (Lat.29°00'N; Long. 77°18'E) was notified vide notification no. PN.10699 dated 08.05.1918. Located in between railway line and NH-1.

Kos Minars Notified in Year 1919

35. **Alapur**, Faridabad kos minar (Lat.29° 02'N; Long. 77°01'E) was notified vide notification no. PN.6798 dated 11.03.1919. Located in between 54-55 milestones before Delhi. At the base portion a little damage can be seen.
36. **Aurangabad**, Faridabad kos minar (Lat.28° 02'N; Long. 77°20'E) was notified vide notification no. PN.6798 dated 11.03.1919. Located before Palwal; to the West of NH-2.
37. **Banchchari I**, Faridabad kos minar (Lat.27°55'N; Long. 77°21'E) was notified vide notification no. PN.6798 dated 11.03.1919. Located 3 km North of Hodal and West of NH-2.
38. **Banchchari II**, Faridabad kos minar (Lat.27°57'N; Long. 77°21'E) was notified vide notification no. PN.6798 dated 11.03.1919. Located 21 km before Palwal and 0.5 km West of NH-2.
39. **Bhulwana**, Faridabad kos minar (Lat.27°52'N; Long. 77°24'E) was notified vide notification no. PN.6798 dated 11.03.1919. Located 4 km before Hodal and East of NH-2. Its tapering part is comparatively short and thick.
40. **Gudhpuri**, Faridabad kos minar (Lat.28°15'N; Long. 77°18'E) was notified vide notification no. PN.6798 dated 11.03.1919.

41. **Gudhpuri (Miranpur),** Faridabad kos minar (Lat.28°13'N; Long. 77°18'E) was notified vide notification no. PN.6798 dated 11.03.1919.
42. **Hodal**, Faridabad kos minar (Lat.27°54'N; Long. 77°23'E) was notified vide notification no. PN.6798 dated 11.03.1919. It is not traceable now (Parihar, 2008:128).
43. **Khateila,** Faridabad kos minar (Lat.28°00'N; Long. 77°20'E) was notified vide notification no. PN.6798 dated 11.03.1919. It is located before Palwal and to the west of NH-2.
44. **Kher Sarai (Phulwari/Bamni Khera),** Faridabad kos minar (Lat.28°04'N; Long. 77°21'E) was notified vide notification no. PN.6798 dated 11.03.1919. Located 9km before Palwal and west of NH-2.
45. **Khusropur (Khuslipur),** Faridabad kos minar (Lat.28°06'N; Long. 77°20'E) was notified vide notification no. PN.6798 dated 11.03.1919. Located 4km before Palwal. Its brick work has been damaged at several parts.
46. **Khwaza Sarai**, Faridabad kos minar (Lat.28°27'N; Long. 78°19'E) was notified vide notification no. PN.6798 dated 11.03.1919. Located in Ashoka Enclave Phase III.
47. **Mawai (Old Faridabad),** Faridabad kos minar (Lat.28°25'N; Long. 77°20'E) was notified vide notification no. PN.6798 dated 11.03.1919. It is located in Sector 29, near market, Old Faridabad.
48. **Mujessar (Ballabhgarh),** Faridabad kos minar (Lat.28°22'N; Long. 77°20'E) was notified vide notification no. PN.6798 dated 11.03.1919. Now Extinct. Originally it was located in plot 113/14A, Sector 24, which is now occupied by a factory, locally known as *Kambalwali Factory* (Parihar, 2008:136).
49. **Palwal, Faridabad** kos minar (Lat.20°09'N; Long. 77°20'E) was notified vide notification no. PN.6798 dated 11.03.1919.
50. **Sikri (Ballabhgarh),** Faridabad kos minar (Lat.28°17'N; Long. 77°18'E) was notified vide notification no. PN.6798 dated 11.03.1919. Located 17 km after Palwal and 6 km before Ballabhgarh; west of NH-2.

PUNJAB

Kos Minars Notified in Year 1921

1. **Ghungrali Rajputan (Khanna),** Ludhiana kos minar (Lat.30°43'N; Long. 76°07'E) was notified vide notification no. PN.24847 dated 14.10.1921. Located about 1.5 km outside of the village. Now, part of its base only exists.

2. **Lashkari Khan (Kot Panaich),** Ludhiana kos minar (Lat.30°45'N; Long. 76°05'E) was notified vide notification no. PN.24847 dated 14.10.1921. Its octagonal part is comparatively high. Located about 100 m away from NH-1; on the road to village Panech and 7km before village Doraha.
3. **Dhandari Kalan**, Ludhiana kos minar (Lat.30°55'N; Long. 75°53'E) was notified vide notification no. PN.24847 dated 14.10.1921.
4. **Sherpur Kalan**, Ludhiana kos minar (Lat.30°54'N; Long. 75°53'E) was notified vide notification no. PN.24847 dated 14.10.1921. Located near Samrala Chowk which now forms a part of Ludhiana City.
5. **Sunnahwal/Sanehwal**, Ludhiana kos minar (Lat.30°50'N; Long.75°59'E) was notified vide notification no. PN.24847 dated 14.10.1921. Located inside the Government High School boundary. Its octagonal part is comparatively high and now is partly damaged.

Kos Minars Notified in Year 1924

6. **Bir Pind (Nakodar),** Jalandhar kos minar (Lat.31°07'N; Long. 75°31'E) was notified vide notification no. PN. 11078 dated 09.04.1924. Located in fields.
7. **Cheema Kalan**, Jalandhar kos minar (Lat.31°65'N; Long. 75°36'E) was notified vide notification no. PN. 11078 dated 09.04.1924. Located about 50 m N of Phillaur-Nurmahal Road.
8. **Dakhni Jahangir**, Jalandhar kos minar (Lat.31°10'N; Long. 75°25'E) was notified vide notification no. PN. 11078 dated 09.04.1924.
9. **Nakodar,** Jalandhar kos minar (Lat.31°08'N; Long. 75°29'E) was notified vide notification no. PN. 11078 dated 09.04.1924. Located in street adjoining Bus stand. Its upper part is comparatively pointed.
10. **Shampur (Nurmahal),** Jalandhar kos minar (Lat.31°05'N; Long. 75°39'E) was notified vide notification no. PN. 11078 dated 09.04.1924. Located in fields.
11. **Tut,** Jalandhar kos minar (Lat.31°09'N; Long. 75°26'E) was notified vide notification no. PN. 11078 dated 09.04.1924. Located to the north of Nakodar-Dakhni Road.
12. **Upal,** Jalandhar kos minar (Lat.31°06'N; Long. 75°34'E) was notified vide notification no. PN. 11078 dated 09.04.1924. Located in the field.
13. **Dakhni** (Dhada Khanpur), Jalandhar kos minar (Lat.31°11'N; Long. 75°22'E) was notified vide notification no. PN. 2031 dated 09.04.1924. Located in the fields.

RAJASTHAN

Kos Minars Notified in Year 1921

1. **Ajmer (S.P. Bunglow)** kos minar (Lat.26°27'N; Long. 74°37'E) was notified vide notification no. AJ.2048 –S dated 10.08.1921. It is situated in rocky terrain dotted with low hills.
2. **Bhunasar,** Ajmer kos minar (Lat.26°28'N; Long. 74°40'E) was notified vide notification no. AJ.2048 –S dated 10.08.1921. Located 135 feet to the right of Ajmer-Jaipur road
3. **Chatri/Chhatri,** Ajmer kos minar (Lat.26°34'N; Long. 74°42'E) was notified vide notification no. AJ.2048 –S dated 10.08.1921.
4. **Ghugra,** Ajmer kos minar (Lat.26°30'N; Long. 74°41'E) was notified vide notification no. AJ.2048 –S dated 10.08.1921. Located 365 feet to the left of the road leading to Kair village.
5. **Hushiara I**, Ajmer kos minar (Lat.26°38'N; Long. 74°45'E) was notified vide notification no. AJ.2048 –S dated 10.08.1921. Located 1.60 km south of village.
6. **Hushiara II**, Ajmer kos minar (Lat.26°36'N; Long. 74°44'E) was notified vide notification no. AJ.2048 –S dated 10.08.1921. Located about half km north of village.
7. **Kair**, Ajmer kos minar (Lat.26°32'N; Long. 74°41'E) was notified vide notification no. AJ.2048 –S dated 10.08.1921. Located about 1km north of village Kair.
8. **Khanpura/Kayamprua**, Ajmer kos minar (Lat.26°35'N; Long. 74°43'E) was notified vide notification no. AJ.2048 –S dated 10.08.1921. Located about 1km north-east of village.

UTTAR PRADESH

Kos Minars Notified in Year 1918

1. **Jarhaulia**, Auraiya kos minar (field no.194/1/(191/1)) was notified vide notification no. UP 653-M 756 dated 05-06-1918.
2. **Paighambarpur**, Auraiya kos minar (field no.215/1)) was notified vide notification no. UP 653-M 756 dated 05-06-1918.
3. **Bhagautipur**, Auraiya kos minar (field no.121) was notified vide notification no. UP 653-M 756 dated 05-06-1918.
4. **Salempur/Sale**, under revenue *mauza* Panhar, Auraiya kos minar (field no.684, 685) was notified vide notification no. UP 653-M 756 dated 05-06-1918.

5. **Gaur** under *tehsil* Bhognipur, Kanpur Dehat kos minar (Lat.26°12'N; Long. 79°51'E) was notified vide notification no. UP 817–M/756 dated 26.07.1918. It is made of lakhauri bricks, lime plastered and circular in plan. Architecturally it is wide at the base and slightly tapering towards the top. Two rows of square perforations exist around the neck portion of the minar.
6. **Gaur** under *taluk* Bhognipur, Kanpur Dehat kos minar (Lat.26°12'N; Long. 79°51'E) was notified vide notification no. UP 817–M/756 dated 26.07.1918. It is wide at the base and slightly tapering towards the top. Two rows of square perforations exist around the neck portion of the minar.
7. **Jalapur Sikandara** under *taluk* Bhognipur, Kanpur Dehat kos minar (Lat.26°22'N; Long. 79°31'E) was notified vide notification no. UP 817–M/756 dated 26.07.1918. It is wide at base and tapering towards top.
8. **Pailwaru** under *taluk* Bhognipur, Kanpur Dehat kos minar (Lat.26°81'N; Long. 79°41'E) was notified vide notification no. UP 817–M/756 dated 26.07.1918. It is wide at the base and slightly tapering towards the top. Its uppermost conical portion is missing but two rows of square perforations exist around the neck part.
9. **Pitampur** under *taluk* Bhognipur, Kanpur Dehat kos minar (Lat.26°23'N; Long. 79°36'E) was notified vide notification no. UP 817–M/756 dated 26.07.1918. It is wide at base and slightly tapering towards the top. Its uppermost conical portion is missing but two rows of square perforations exist around the neck part.
10. **Rajpur** under *taluk* Bhognipur, Kanpur Dehat kos minar (Lat.26°16'N; Long. 79°40'E) was notified vide notification no. UP 817–M/756 dated 26.07.1918. It is wide at the base and slightly tapering towards the top.
11. **Sankhin Buzurg** under *taluk* Sikandara, Kanpur Dehat kos minar (Lat.26°23'N; Long. 79°37'E) was notified vide notification no. UP 817–M/756 dated 26.07.1918. It it is wide at the base and slightly tapering towards the top. Two rows of square perforations exist around the neck portion of the minar.
12. **Sardarpur** under *taluk* Sikandara, Kanpur Dehat kos minar (Lat.26°20'N; Long. 79°44'E) was notified vide notification no. UP 817–M/756 dated 26.07.1918. It is wide at the base and conical part has been damaged. Two rows of square perforations exist around the neck portion of the minar.
13. **Bhognipur I**, Kanpur Dehat kos minar was notified vide notification no. UP 817 –M/756 dated 26.07.1918. Details are not available.

14. **Bhognipur II**, Kanpur Dehat kos minar was notified vide notification no. UP 817 –M/756 dated 26.07.1918. Details are not available.
15. **Chaparghata** under *tehsil* Bhognipur, Kanpur Dehat kos minar was notified vide notification no. UP 817–M/756 dated 26.07.1918. Details are not available.
16. **Deosar** under *tehsil* Ghatampur, Kanpur Dehat kos minar was notified vide notification no. UP 817–M/756 dated 26.07.1918. Details are not available.
17. **Halia** under *tehsil* Ghatampur, Kanpur Dehat kos minar was notified vide notification no. UP 817–M/756 dated 26.07.1918. Details are not available.
18. **Raigwan** under *tehsil* Bhognipur, Kanpur Dehat kos minar was notified vide notification no. UP 817–M/756 dated 26.07.1918. Details are not available.
19. **Khalispur** under *tehsil* Bhognipur, Kanpur Dehat kos minar was notified vide notification no. UP 817–M/756 dated 26.07.1918. Details are not available.

Kos Minars Notified in Year 1920

20. **Sarai**, Agra kos minar (Mile 09 Furlong 04) was notified vide notification no. UP 1645-M/1133 dated 22-12-1920. Located on Agra-Fatehpur Sikri Road.
21. **Midhakur**, Agra kos minar (Mile11 Furlong 01) was notified vide notification no. UP 1645-M/1133 dated 22-12-1920. Located on Agra-Fatehpur Sikri Road.
22. **Mahuar**, Agra kos minar (Mile12 Furlong 07) was notified vide notification no. UP 1645-M/1133 dated 22-12-1920. Located on Agra-Fatehpur Sikri Road.
23. **Kiraoli**, Agra kos minar (Mile15 Furlong 02) was notified vide notification no. UP 1645-M/1133 dated 22-12-1920. Located on Agra-Fatehpur Sikri Road.
24. **Halwai ki Bahgichi** (near Mental Hospital), Agra kos minar (Mile 04 Furlong 03) was notified vide notification no. UP 1645-M/1133 dated 22-12-1920. Located on Agra-Mathura Road.
25. **Sikandra** (near Sudhir Dharamkanta), Agra kos minar (Mile 06 Furlong 07) was notified vide notification no. UP 1645-M/1133 dated 22-12-1920. Located on Agra-Mathura Road. Its top is crowned with amalaka shaped finial.

26. **Sherjung Baba ki Mazar**, Agra kos minar (Mile 09 Furlong 04) was notified vide notification no. UP 1645-M/1133 dated 22-12-1920. Located on Agra-Mathura Road.
27. **Runukta**, Agra kos minar (Mile 12 Furlong 01) was notified vide notification no. UP 1645-M/1133 dated 22-12-1920. Located on Agra-Mathura Road.
28. **Chhatta Main Road**, Mathura kos minar (Mile 19 Furlong 01) was notified vide notification no. UP 1645-M/1133 dated 22-12-1920.
29. **Azizpur (Chhatta)**, Mathura kos minar (Mile 24 Furlong 03) was notified vide notification no. UP 1645-M/1133 dated 22-12-1920. There is a ring moulding in the middle of cylindrical part.
30. **Kosi Kalna (Chhatta)**, Mathura kos minar (Mile 26 Furlong 07) was notified vide notification no. UP 1645-M/1133 dated 22-12-1920.
31. **Kotban (Chhatta)**, Mathura kos minar (Mile 29 Furlong 04) was notified vide notification no. UP 1645-M/1133 dated 22-12-1920. This is the last kos minar of Uttar Pradesh and located 8 km before Hodal, Haryana.
32. **Mathura** kos minar, located on the circular road was notified vide notification no. UP 1645-M/1133 dated 22-12-1920.
33. **Muniara** Mathura kos minar, (Mile 03 Furlong 5.17) was notified vide notification no. UP 1645-M/1133 dated 22-12-1920. Located to south of the village and 6km NW of Mathura.
34. **Chamah/Chaumuha**, Mathura kos minar, (Mile 11 Furlong 5) notified vide notification no. UP 1645-M/1133 dated 22-12-1920. Located west of the village (72 km NW of Agra) on Mathura-Delhi Road, NH-2.
35. **Akbarpur**, Mathura kos minar, (opposite to Mile 13 Furlong 1 from road) was notified vide notification no. UP 1645-M/1133 dated 22-12-1920. Located on Mathura-Delhi road; 8 km before Chhata and 19 km before Kosi. Damaged at base portion.
36. **Nai Semri** Mathura kos minar, (Mile 116, Yards 400 from road) was notified vide notification no. UP 1645-M/1133 dated 22-12-1920.
37. **Kos Minar near Bhootnath Temple**, in the beginning of Dig road was notified vide notification no. UP 1645-M/1133 dated 22-12-1920. Located on Mathura-Dig road.

Kos Minars Notified in Year 1942

38. **Gohari**, Mathura kos minar was notified vide notification no. Edlands F.0401(2)/42-F &L dated 26-01-1942.

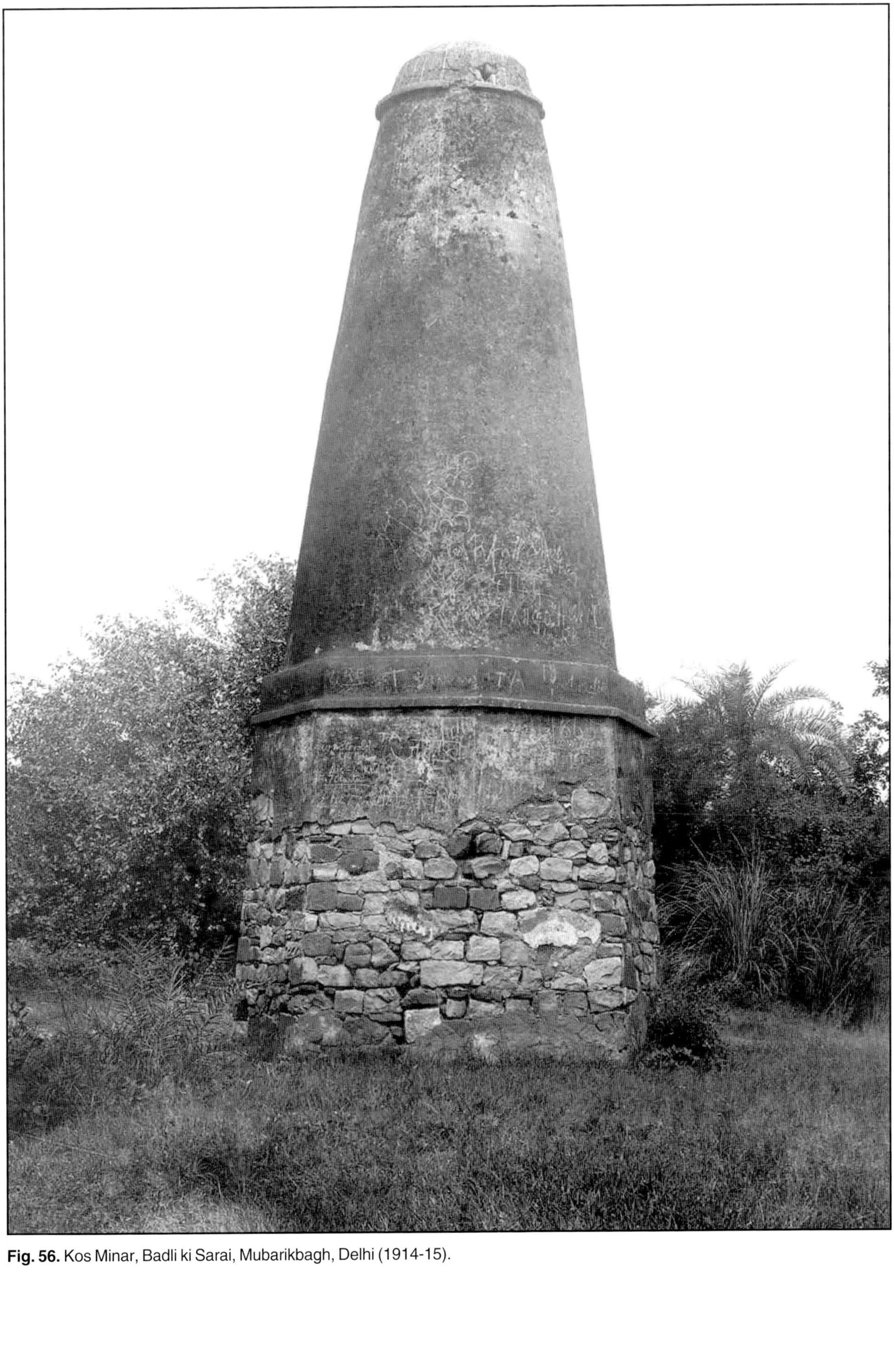

Fig. 56. Kos Minar, Badli ki Sarai, Mubarikbagh, Delhi (1914-15).

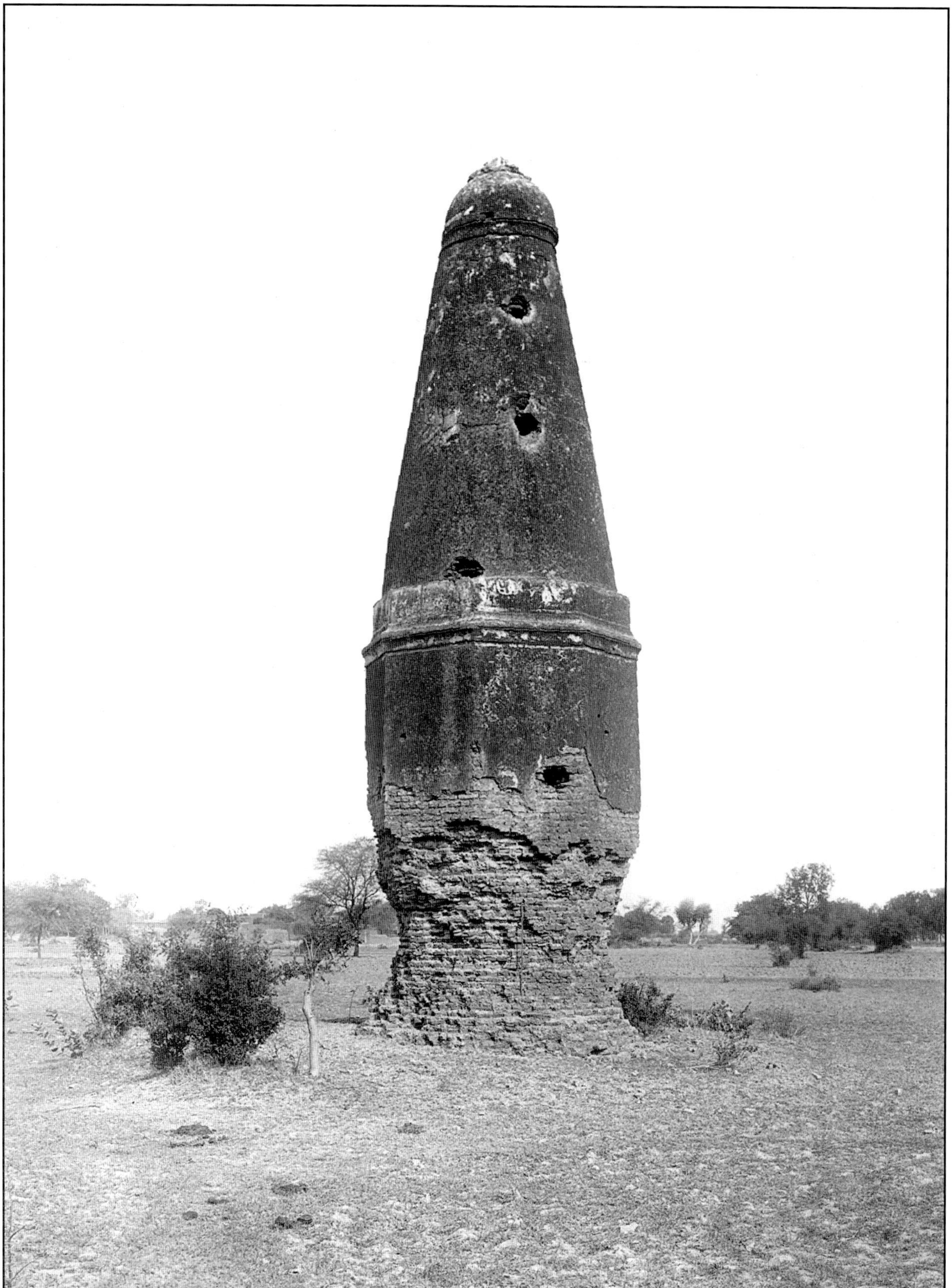

Fig. 57. Kos Minar, Sirhind, general view (1911-13).

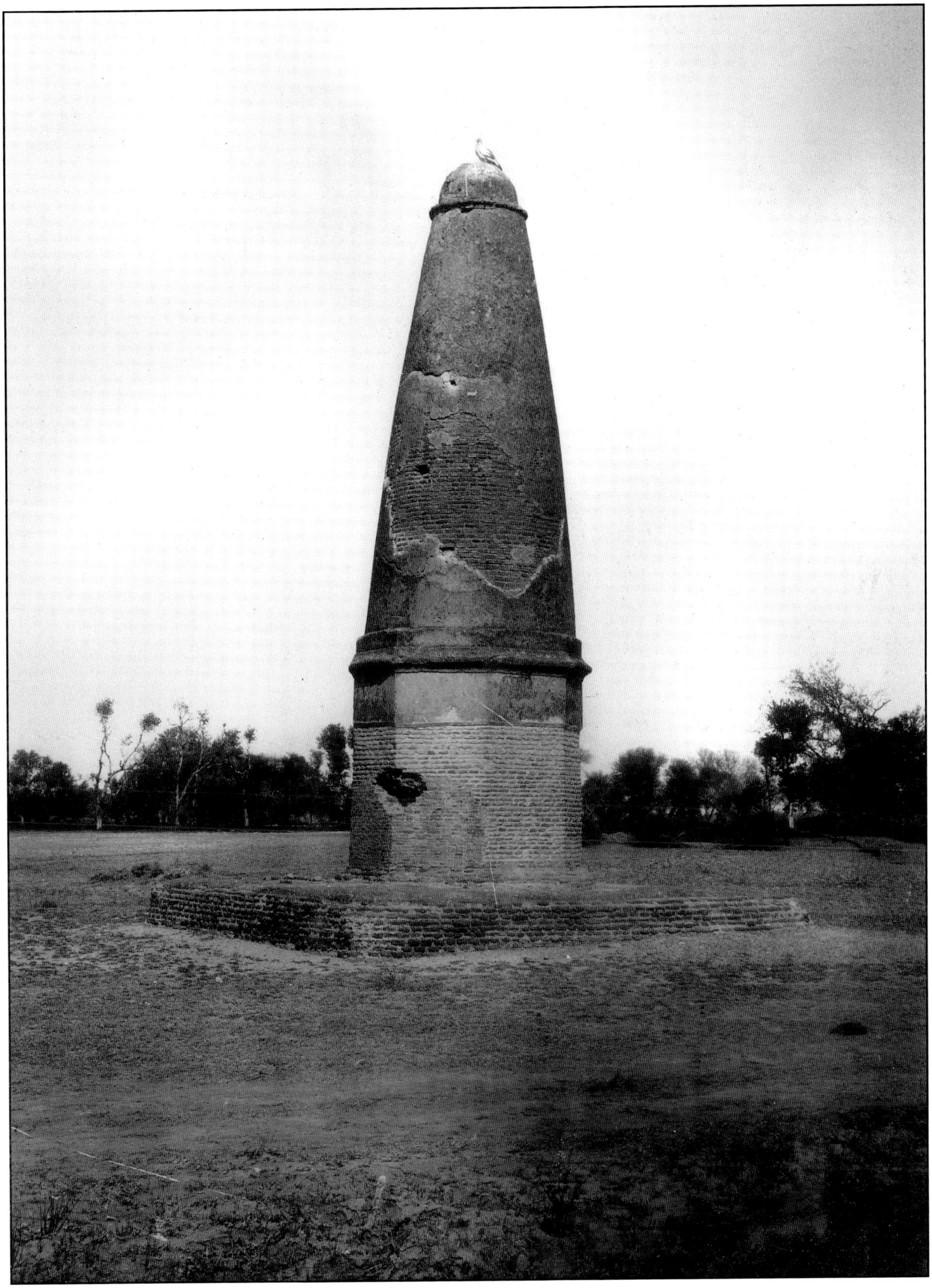

Fig. 58. Dakhni Sarai Kos Minar No. 1, Nakodar (1936-37).

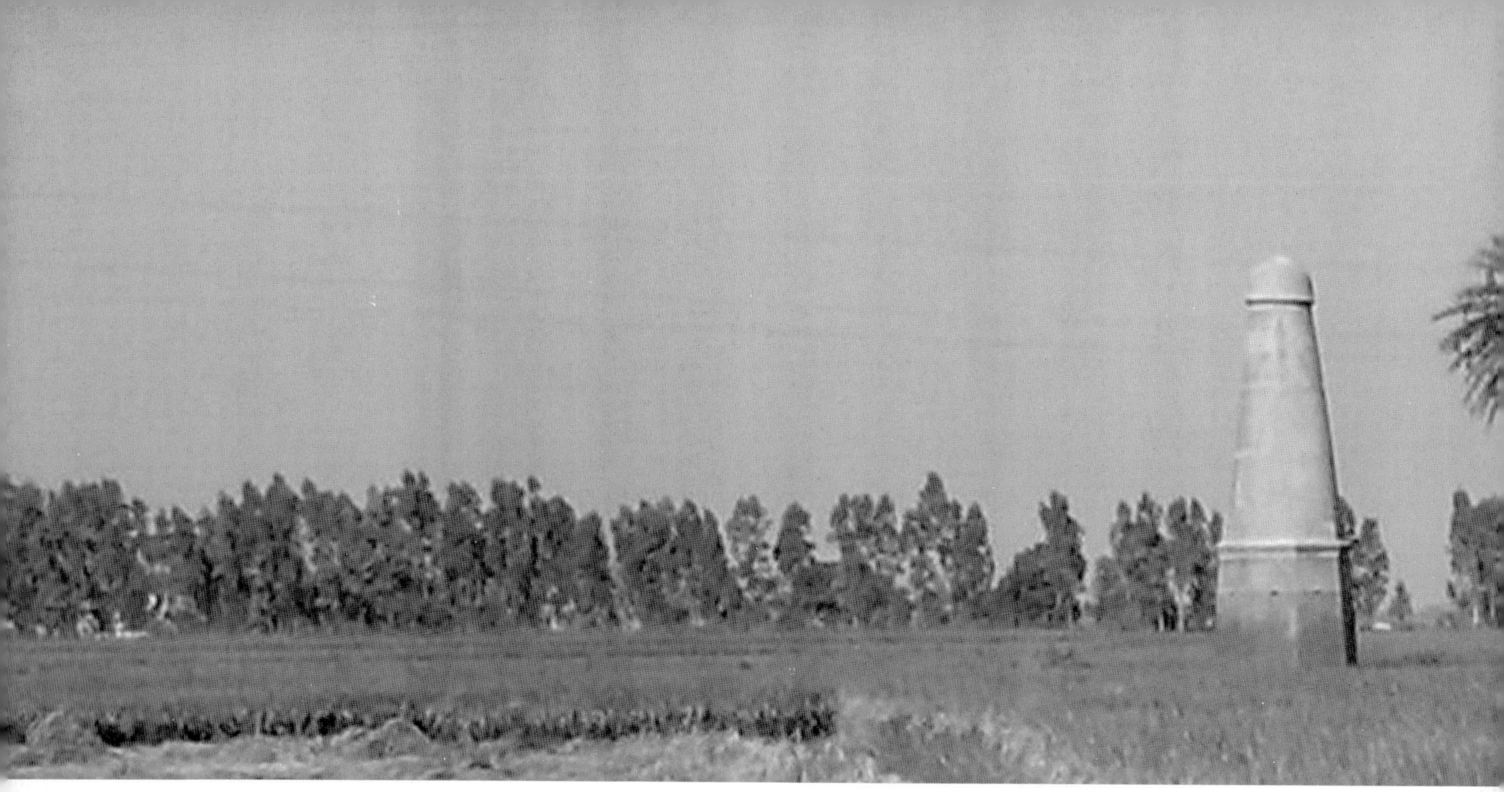

Appendix II

List of Protected Kos Minars in Haryana

(Under Chandigarh Circle)

Sr. No.	Name	Location	Height	Thickness	Width	Base/Platform
1.	Bhulwana	Agra-Delhi road, about 150 m right side of road and 1½km SE of village.	10.30 m	1.20 m	1.20 m	Square 6.40 sq.m
2.	Hodal	In between village Hodal.	10.30 m	1.20 m	1.20 m	Square
3.	Banchari-I	Left hand side of Agra-Delhi road at about 200 m 1 km SE of village.	10.30 m	—	—	Square
4.	Banchari-II	500 m west of Agra-Delhi road near 80 km milestone. No approach road to Kos minar.	—	—	—	Square
5.	Khatela	On left hand side of main road.	—	—	—	Square
6.	Aurangabad	Left hand side of Agra-Delhi road.	—	—	—	Square

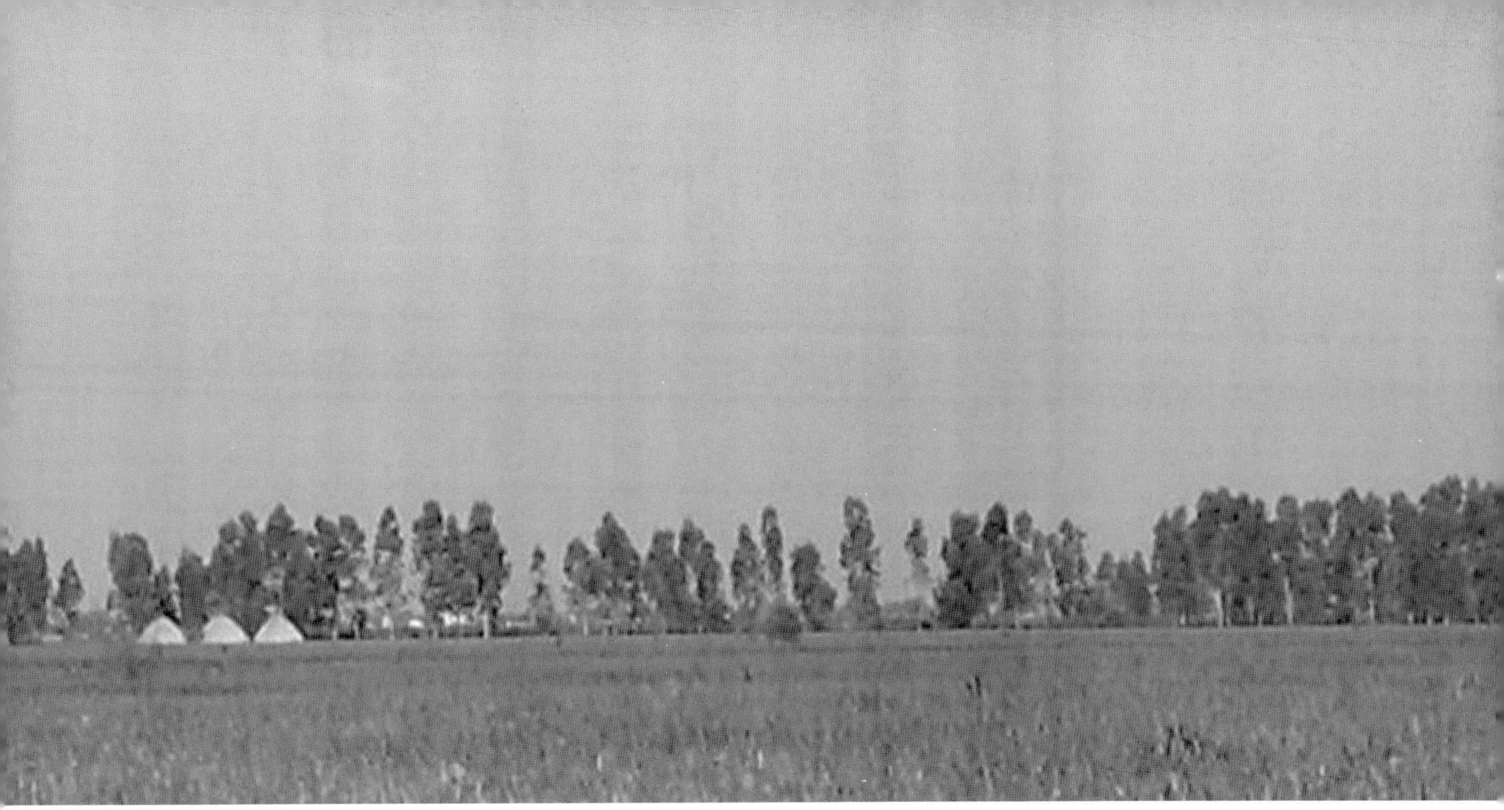

Shaft	T x H	Top	Bldg. Material	Mortar	Plaster	Features	Decoration	Present Condition
Octagonal	1.20 m x 3.30 m	Convex-tapering with 7 m ring	Lakhori bricks	Lime-Surkhi-Sand	Lime-Surkhi-Sand	2 string course, bulgy, sharp curve.	Moulding on extreme top.	Good. Surrounded by heavy growth of vegetation.
Octagonal	1.2 x 3.3 m	Convex-tapering	"	"	"	2 string course, bulgy, sharp curve, pointed-plastered.	—	Well preserved.
Octagonal	– x 3.3 m	Convex-tapering with 7 m ring	"	"	"		—	Plattorm filled with debris shaft damaged.
Octagonal		Elongated	"	"	"	2 string course, elongated.	—	De-plastered at places. Shaft portion is in very bad condition. Surrounded by growth of vegetation.
Octagonal		Straight tapering elongated	"	"	"	2 string course.	—	Shaft portion damaged. a lot. Growth of vegetation all around.
Octagonal		Straight tapering	"	"	"	2 string course, conical.	—	De-plastering and development of area is required.

Sr. No.	Name	Location	Height	Thickness	Width	Base/Platform
7.	Bhamni-Kheda	Left hand side of main road and north of village on Phulwani Link road.	—	—	—	Square
8.	Kosalipur or Khusropur	Right hand side of main road and SE of village.	—	—	—	Square
9.	Palwal	Right hand side of road in between the city near shop of Rajkumar.	—	—	—	Square
10.	Alapur	In between the village within house of Kirpa s/o Bhup Singh.	—	—	—	Square
11.	Miranpur or Gudhpuri No. 1	Left hand side of the main road in between fields.	—	—	—	Square
12.	Gudhpuri No. 2	200 m from main road behind HSIDC complex.	—	—	—	Square
13.	Sikri	150 m left of Agra-Delhi road.	—	—	—	Square
14.	Mawai	Sect. 29 of Faridabad on right hand side of the road.	—	—	—	Square
15.	Ghosipur Sarai	Sect. 35 of Faridabad near water tank and Tolstoy school.	—	—	—	Square
16.	Badarpur	Right hand side of the main road.	—	—	—	Square
17.	Akbarpura Barota	Situated on Sonepat-Narela road and 1 km SE of village.	—	—	—	Square
18.	Jagdishpur	Left side of the road in between feilds.	—	—	—	Square
19.	Baiyanpur	Situated on left hand side of Sonepat-Narela road, 400 m in between fields.	—	—	—	Square 1 m
20.	Sonepat City	Near Bus Stand	—	—	—	Square

Shaft	T x H	Top	Bldg. Material	Mortar	Plaster	Features	Decoration	Present Condition
Octagonal		Convex tapering	"	"	"	2 string course, bulgy at bottom.	—	Enclosed in grilled fencing. De-plastering at places. Good condition.
Octagonal		Tapering	"	"	"	2 string course, bulgy at bottom & pointed at top.	—	Enclosed in grilled fencing. Heavy growth of vegetation.
Octagonal		Slight tapering	"	"	"	2 string course, conical from bottom to top.	—	Encroached by shop. Deplastered at places. Bad condition of shaft portion.
Octagonal		Tapering	"	"	"	2 string course, like Palwal.	—	Encroached by house. Deplastered. Shaft portion is badly damaged.
Octagonal		Tapering	"	"	"	2 string course, bulgy at bottom.	—	Good state of preservation. Growth of vegetation all around.
Octagonal		Convex tapering	"	"	"	"	—	"
Octagonal		Tapering	"	"	"	2 string course, conical from bottom to top.	—	Deplastering at places. Shaft portion fully deplastered.
Octagonal		Tapering	"	"	"	"	—	Replaced into a temple and white-washed. Totally encroached.
Octagonal		Tapering	"	"	"	"	—	Bricks replaced by stones. Good condition.
Octagonal		Conical	Stone is complete	Lime-Surkhi-Sand	Lime-Surkhi-Sand	2 string course, bulky tapering.	—	Encroached by Sh. Ram Singh. Deplastering at the shaft portion.
Octagonal		Tapering	Lakhori bricks	"	"	2 string course, bulky bottom.	—	Shaft is in bad condition. Growth of vegetation all over
Octagonal		Tapering	"	"	"	2 string course, tapering.	—	Growth of vegetation all over. Good state.
Octagonal		Tapering	"	"	"	2 string course, straight upto shaft & tapering above.	—	Shaft is heavily damaged & growth of vegetation.
Octagonal		Tapering	"	"	"	2 string course, bulgy.	—	Encroached by Sh. Suresh Kr. s/o Vipendra Kr. Half of shaft & full of base has gone below modern road. Shaft in bad condition.

Sr. No.	Name	Location	Height	Thickness	Width	Base/Platform
21.	Jawahari	On Sonepat-Rajpur-Ganam road on left side.	9.90 m	—	—	Square 5.6 x 6.6
22.	Rajpur	SW of village near railway track.	—	—	—	Square
23.	Jatipur	Near house of Shri Prabhu Dayal s/o Sh. Risal Singh.	—	—	—	—
24.	Panipat No. 1	SE of Panipat and opposite to Khadi Ashram	—	—	—	Square
25.	Panipat No. 2.	In Mohalla Jawahar Nagar, near house of Sh. Mohan Kr. s/o Inder Bhan, and Tarachand s/o Sh. Shankar	—	—	—	Square
26.	Kohand	Right hand side of G.T. Road.	—	—	—	Square
27.	Gharaunda (N)	1.5 km north of village in between fields.	—	—	—	Square
28.	Gharaunda (s)	Left hand side of G.T. Road, about 2 km south of town.	—	—	—	Square
29.	Kutail	Right side of G.T. Road.	—	—	—	Square
30.	Daha	On G.T. Road, near Madhuban Police Station.	—	—	—	Square
31.	Karnal No. 1	Right hand side of G.T. Road and SE of city near Namaste Chowk.	—	—	—	Square
32.	Karnal No. 2	Right hand side of G.T. Road, near boundary of Govt. Dairy Farm.	2.35 m	—	—	Square
33.	Behni-Kalan	1 km from village.	—	—	—	Square

Shaft	T x H	Top	Bldg. Material	Mortar	Plaster	Features	Decoration	Present Condition
Octagonal		Convex tapering	"	"	"	2 string course, bulgy till top.	—	Bad condition of the shaft. Deplastering at places.
Octagonal		Tapering conically	"	"	"	2 string course, bulgy at bottom but more conical at top.	—	Deplastering. Still in good condition.
Octagonal		Convex tapering	"	"	"	2 string course, bulgy.	—	—
Octagonal		Tapering	"	"	"	2 string course, bulgy.	—	Good state of preservation. However lower portion of shaft and base in full has been covered by debris & vegetation all around. Heavily encroached in surrounding areas. Growth of vegetation all-round.
Octagonal		Tapering	"	"	"	2 string course, bulgy at bottom.	—	Converted into Shivara Temple. Good state of preservation.
Octagonal		Tapering	"	"	"	2 string course, bulgy at bottom.	—	Enclosed within grill fencing. Renovated fully at shaft portion. Good state.
Octagonal		Tapering	"	"	"	2 string course, bulgy, straight sided shaft.	—	Good state of preservation. Growth of vegetation all around.
Octagonal		Convex tapering	Lakhori bricks	Lime-Surkhi-Sand	Lime-Surkhi-Sand	2 string course, bulgy all over.	—	Good state of preservation. Enclosed within a newly built enclosure wall.
Octagonal		Convex tapering	"	"	"	2 string course, bulgy all over.	—	Good state of preservation. Renovated at parts.
Octagonal		Convex tapering	"	"	"	2 string course, very bulgy.	—	Enclosed within grilled fence. Good state. Renovated at parts.
Octagonal		Tapering	"	"	"	2 string course, bulgy top.	—	Good state. Renovated at portion.
Octagonal		—	—	—	—	—	—	—
Octagonal		Convex tapering	"	"	"	2 string course, bulgy.	—	Extreme top is broken off. Shaft is in broken condition too. Growth of vegetation all over.

Sr. No.	Name	Location	Height	Thickness	Width	Base/Platform
34.	Taraori (S)	SW of village, near Anaj Mandi.	—	—	—	Square
35.	Taraori (N)	NW of village.	—	—	—	Square
36.	Amin	On Amin-Barthal road. South of village about 2.5 km away.	—	—	—	Square
37.	Fatuhpur	2 km NW of village Amin	—	—	—	Square
38.	Dara Kalan (Thanesar)	SW of village on Thanesar-Salaorpur road, behind Singha Rice Mill.	—	—	—	Square
39.	Bhiwani-Khera	2.5 km from Sheikh Chilli's tomb on Thanesar-Jhansa road.	—	—	—	Square
40.	Adhon	1.5 km north of village on Adon-Adhoni road.	—	—	—	Square
41.	Sarai Sukhi	NE of Dhirpur railway station.	—	—	—	Square
42.	Zainpura	100 m right of G.T. Road and 4.5 km from Shahbad city.	—	—	—	Square
43.	Mohri	200 m left side of G.T. Road.	7.0 m	—	—	Square
44.	Muchchaunda	NW of village near brick kiln of Gian Chand.	5.15 m	—	—	Square
45.	Ambala City	On B.S. to railway station road, near shop of Chunnilal Roshanlal Cloth Merchant.	—	—	—	Square

Shaft	T x H	Top	Bldg. Material	Mortar	Plaster	Features	Decoration	Present Condition
Octagonal		Straight tapering	"	"	"	2 string course, bulgy, extreme top has a knob protruding.	—	Good condition. Renovated fully.
Octagonal		Straight tapering	"	"	"	2 string course, bulgy, extreme top has a knob protruding.	—	Good condition. Deplastering at shaft portion.
Octagonal		Tapering slightly	"	"	"	2 string course, bulgy body all over, conical extreme top.	—	Good state of preservation. Renovated in full.
Octagonal		Tapering	"	"	"	2 string course, straight upto shaft but tapers more on top.	—	Deplastered at parts. Shaft is in bad condition. Growth of vegetation all over.
Octagonal		Tapering	"	"	"	2 string course.	—	Bad state. Deplastering at places. Growth of vegetation and trees all around.
Octagonal		Tapering	"	"	"	2 string course, straight shaft & conical top.	—	Renovated fully. Good state.
Octagonal		Tapering	"	"	"	2 string course.	—	Renovated fully.
Octagonal		Tapering	Lakhori bricks	Lime-Surkhi-Sand	Lime-Surkhi-Sand	2 string course, inlay work at the mouldings, straight shaft but tapering top.	—	Deplastered at places. Shaft is in bad condition.
Octagonal		Tapering	"	"	"	2 string course.	—	Very bad state. Shaft is damaged fully. Growth of vegetation and trees all around.
Round		Tapering	"	"	"	Single string course, straight tapering.	—	Very bad condition.
Octagonal		Dia 7 m tapering	"	"	"	2 string course, straight tapering	—	Shaft is in very bad state.
*Round		Tapering	"	"	"	Single string course. Straight up to a limit and tapering upwards.	—	De-plastered, renovated partially

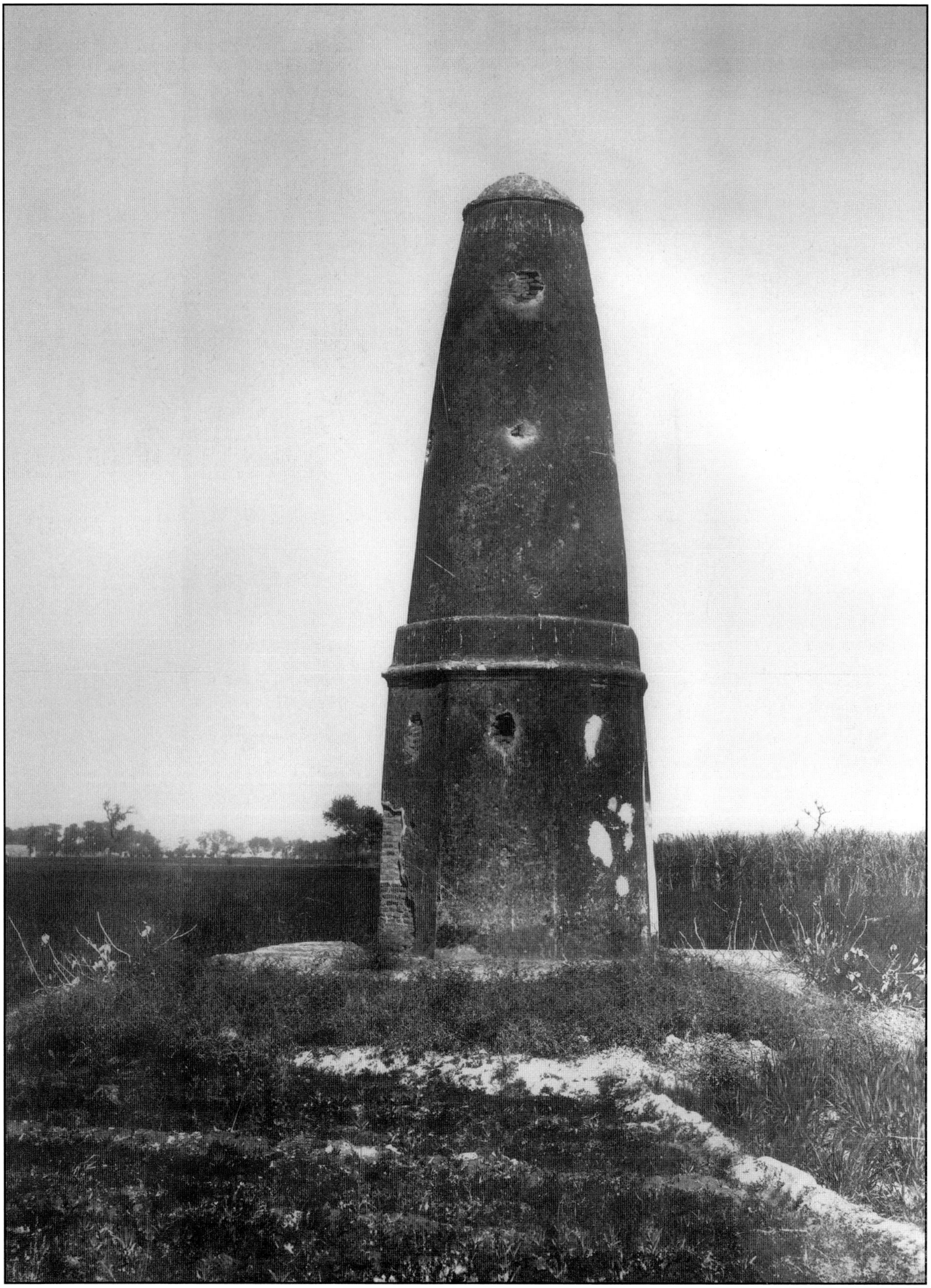

Fig. 59. Noor Mahal Kos Minar No. 4 before clearance of jungle, Nakodar (1936-37).

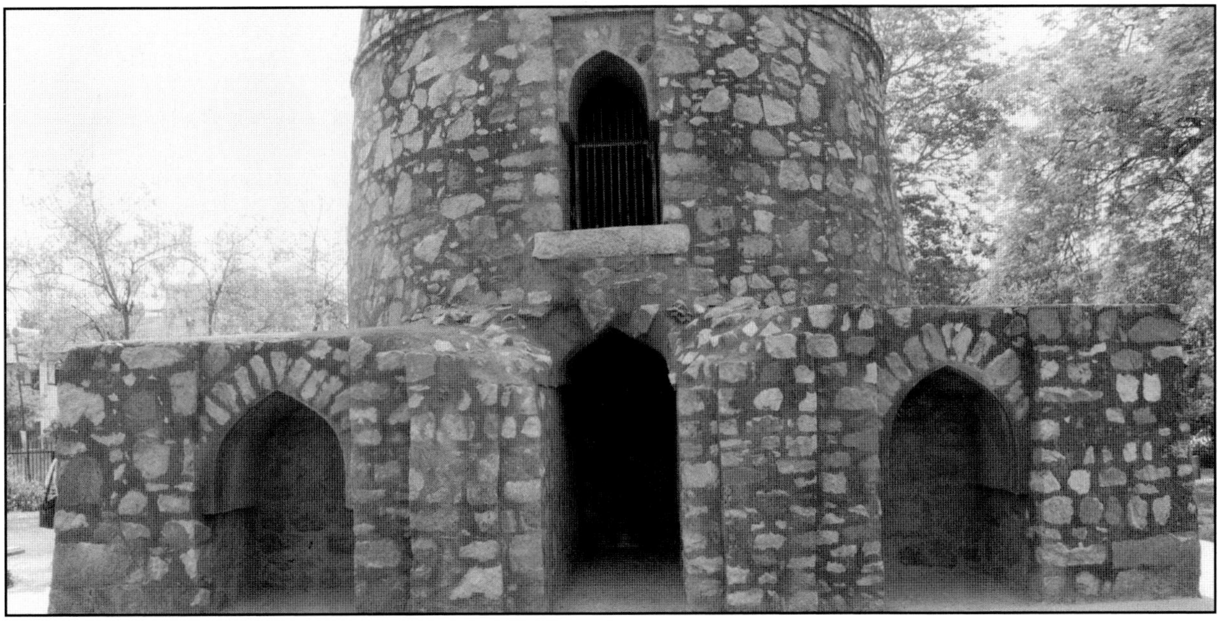

Bibliography

Chandra, Moti. 1977. *Trade and Trade Routes in Ancient India*. Abhinav Publications, New Delhi.

Hasan, Maulvi Zafar. 1922. *Delhi Province, List of Muhammadan and Hindu Monuments, Volume III: Mahrauli Zail*, J.F. Blakiston (ed.). Superintendent, Government Printing, Calcutta. Reprinted in 1997 by Aryan Books International, New Delhi under the title *Monuments of Delhi: Lasting Splendour of the Great Mughals and Others*.

Kanga, Ervad M.F. and N.S. Sontakke (eds.). 1978. *Avesta Part III Vendidad and Fragments.* T.N. Dharmadhikari & H.N. Joshi, Secretaries, Vaidika Samsodhana Mandala, Gultekdi, Poona.

Khan, Abid Ali.1986 (rpt.). *Memoirs of Gaur and Pandua.* Department of Information & Cultural Affairs, Government of West Bengal. (First published in 1931).

Lal, B.B. 2005. *The Homeland of the Aryans, Evidence of Rigvedic Flora & Fauna and Archaeology.* Aryan Books International, New Delhi.

Nath, R. 1999. *Chittorgarh Kirttistambha of Maharana Kumbha (The Idea and The Form) (1440–60 AD).* Abhinav Publications, New Delhi.

Parihar, Subhash. 2008. *Land Transport in Mughal India, Agra Lahore Mughal Highway and its. Architectural Remains.* Aryan Books International, New Delhi.

Sharma, D.V. 2008. *Archaeology of Fatehpur Sikri: New Discoveries*. Aryan Books International, New Delhi.

Sharma, Y.D. 2001. *Delhi And its Neighbourhood*. Archaeological Survey of India, New Delhi.